Illustrations of Bible Truth

by

H.A. Ironside

www.solidchristianbooks.com

www.harryironsidebooks.com

Contents

Preface 5
Doubtful Things.. 6
Discerning Love 6
Evil Communications... 7
He Did His Part.. 7
Help Those Women 8
Passing Trials 9
Lost In The Church.. 10
The Offer Of The Irish Landlord 11
God's Blessed Man... 14
Encouragement To Pray 15
A Negro Preacher On Missions 18
The Preacher And Fried Chicken 19
Milk Your Own Cow 21
The Two Natures.. 23
Honor To Whom Honor Is Due 24
Washing Out The Scent 24
Satisfaction In Christ 26
On Top Of The Beer Barrel 26
"Read Ezekiel 7:8, 9".. 28
The Lord's Spectacles... 29
Accepted In The Beloved 30
Standing Where The Fire Has Been 31
A Victim Of Wrong Information 32
Cobbling For The Glory Of God 35
Blind Leaders Of The Blind 37

Law And Grace 37

The Gift Of God...39

The New Man 40

The Wrong Remedy 41

A Lost Opportunity 44

Example Of New Birth 45

An Arrow Shot At A Venture...46

Possessing Our Possessions...48

The Cleansing Word...49

In The Cleft Of The Rock 51

A Butterfly Used To Answer Prayer..................................52

Only Three Weeks To Live 53

Patriotism-Plus..57

Why The Train Was Wrecked 59

The Hen And The Lizard 60

"Lippen To" Jesus 61

Open The Door To Jesus...62

Who Can Pay? 64

A Good Sinner 67

The Human Fly 68

"I'm In For A Good Time"..69

Not Only Necessary—But Enough 72

The One Mediator 73

The Unsettled Past 75

The Conversion Of Thomas Scott, A Unitarian...............77

No Oil In The Lamp...78

Praying Or Trusting 80

Living The Christ Life	82
Honest Doubt	83
The Blood Counts For Something	84
The Wrong Door	86
Salvation Altogether Of God	87
The Bible A Mirror	88
The Righteousness Of God	90
Total Depravity	91
The Fulness Of The Scriptures	92
Simplicity In Prayer	93
Verbal Inspiration	96
The Ribbon Of Blue	99
Copper Nails	100
Magnifying Christ	102
Holding On To Spikes	105
Possessing Our Possessions	107
The Hands Of The Saviour	109
Hasty Conclusions	111

Preface

I think it was Charles H. Spurgeon who said, "The sermon is the house; the illustrations are the windows that let in the light." Whether this remark was original with him or not, it is very true and deserves to be kept in mind and practically applied by those who would preach the Word in compelling power.

Some object to the use of anecdotes of any kind in preaching and teaching, and think all that is needed is the unfolding of the truth. But most minds are so constituted that they need illustrations to enable them readily to grasp the full import of the message. Our Lord Himself used this method continually and in this, as in other things, He has left "us an example, that ye should follow his steps."

At the request of valued friends, I have grouped together here many stories and incidents which have served me well throughout a long ministry and which I hope may be used to advantage by others. Many are from my own personal experience and will not be found in the collections of other writers. Some, however, have been used in my books on various subjects. Others are now printed for the first time. I send them forth to the glory of Him who has been to me for over half a century, a wonderful Saviour and a faithful Friend, my ever adorable Lord Jesus Christ.

H. A. Ironside

Chicago, Ill.

Doubtful Things

"He that doubteth is condemned if he eat" (Rom. 14:23, R.V.).

Sandy was a thrifty Scot who objected to needless laundry expense, so when he wore a dress shirt to a banquet, he put it away carefully for future use. On one occasion when dressing for such an event, he took a used shirt out of the drawer and examined it with care, hoping to be able to wear it that evening. Not being quite sure of its strict cleanliness, he took it to a window, where he was looking it over under a better light than the room afforded. His wife, Jean, noticed him shaking his head as though fearful that it would not pass careful scrutiny.

"Remember, Sandy," she called to him, "if it's doubtful, it's dirty."

That settled it. The shirt went into the discard and another—a fresh one—took its place. Jean's words may well speak to every believer concerning things about which conscience raises any question whatsoever.

Discerning Love

"That your love may abound ... in all discernment" (Phil. 1:9, literal translation).

Lack of discernment often accounts for the failure of those in the pew to realize the full import of unsound teaching from the pulpit.

A brilliant modernistic preacher, who had pleased his audience with flowery oratory and beautiful perorations, as he discoursed glibly of the importance of breadth of view and the danger of bigoted opinions, was bidding farewell to his congregation as he was about to leave them for a new parish. One of his young men approached him and said, "Pastor, I am so sorry we are losing you. Before you came I was one who did not care for God, man, or the devil, but through your delightful sermons, I have learned to love them all!" This is mere sentimentality—not discerning love.

Evil Communications

"Evil communications corrupt good manners" (I Cor. 15:33).

Roaming in the woods, some boys found a nest containing two linnet fledglings, which they managed to capture and take home. Securing some plain, wooden birdcages, they put one of the linnets in each and hung them on either side of a canary. They explained to their mother that they hoped the linnets, being so young, would learn to imitate the canary, instead of *cheeping* as linnets ordinarily do. The mother smilingly questioned the likelihood of the plan succeeding.

The next day the boys entered the room, and exclaimed, "Mother, come here, our canary is *cheeping* like a linnet!"

And so it was. The canary had to be separated from the wild birds of the wood and kept under cover for a time before he regained his song. Surely there is a lesson here for all Christians. Fellowship with the world does not lead the godless to take the way of the Lord, but generally results in the believer losing his joyous song and taking on the speech and manners of the world.

He Did His Part

'The son of man is come to seek and to save that which was lost" (Luke 19:10).

That man is an utterly lost sinner who could never find his own way back to God, is a very unpalatable truth for the average natural man or woman. We all like to think there is something we can do to help save ourselves, whereas, according to God's Word we are not only lost, but without ability to retrieve our condition. It is remarkable how apt the colored folks are in quick illustrations of spiritual realities, as the following instance will show.

A recent convert, a colored man, rose in a meeting to give his testimony to the saving grace of God. He told how the Lord had won his heart and given deliverance from the guilt and power of sin. He spoke of Christ and His work, but said nothing of any efforts of his own.

The leader of the meeting was of a legalistic turn of mind, and when the negro's testimony was ended, he said, "Our brother has only told us of the Lord's part in his salvation. When I was converted there was a whole lot I had to do myself before I could expect the Lord to do anything for me. Brother, didn't you do your part first before God did His?" The other was on his feet again in an instant and replied: "Yes, sah, Ah clear done forgot. Ah didn't tell you 'bout my part, did I? Well, Ah did my part for over thirty years, runnin' away from God as fast as evah my sins could carry me. That was my part. An' God took aftah me till He run me down. That was His part." It was well put and tells the story that every redeemed sinner understands.

Help Those Women

"And I intreat thee also, true yoke fellow, help those women ..." (Phil. 4:3).

He was unschooled, and trying to give a word of exhortation. He fumbled through the opening verses of Philippians 4, but became confused over the names of the two women referred to in verse 2, and so he read, "I beseech Odious and I beseech Soontouchy that they be of the same mind in the Lord." He then proceeded to attempt an application of the truth according to the names as he had misunderstood them.

How much trouble is made among Christians by women like Odious, who are sounpleasant to get on with, and Soontouchy, who get offended over every little trifle! The application was good, though the interpretation was faulty.

Passing Trials

"Our light affliction, which is but for a moment" (II Cor. 4:17).

He was a very illiterate negro, who could only spell his way through the Bible with great effort and often failed to grasp the full import of the passages he tried to read. Rising to his feet in a testimony meeting where the leader had called upon each one to give his favorite portion of Scripture, the aged, colored brother said, "I gets more help from dem bressed words 'And it came to pass' than anything else in the Bible."

Asked what he meant, he explained, "When I'se so upset wid trouble and pestered wid trials, I goes to the Bible, and begins to read, and I never goes far before I come across dem words, 'It came to pass' and I says, 'Bress de

Lawd. It didn't come to stay. It come to pass!'" Surely we may all learn from his simple faith.

Lost In The Church

"If our gospel be hid, it is hid to them that are lost" (II Cor. 4:3).

In an English village a Sunday school entertainment was being held in a small church. The place was crowded and in darkness as a stereopticon exhibition was being given. A knock at the door summoned an usher, who made his way to the front and announced, "Little Mary Jones is lost. Her family and the town officers have been searching everywhere for her. If anyone has seen her or knows of her whereabouts, will he please go to the door and communicate with the friend who is inquiring." No one moved and the lecturer went on with his address and pictures.

At the close, when the lights were turned on, a lady noticed Mary sitting on a front seat. Going over to her, she said,

"Why, Mary, didn't you hear them inquiring for you? Why did you not let them know you were here?"

Surprised, the child asked, "Did they mean me? They said Mary Jones was lost. I am not lost. I knew where I was all the time; I thought it was some other Mary Jones."

She was lost in the church and did not know it. How many others are like her. They have a name that they live, but are dead. Though members of some local church, they have never seen their need of Christ, nor have they believed the message of the gospel

The Offer Of The Irish Landlord

"I told you, and ye believed not" (John 10:25).

The unwillingness of the human heart to rely on the promise of grace in Christ Jesus is well illustrated in the story of an eccentric Irish landlord on whose vast estates dwelt a number of very needy tenants. Upon becoming converted, this wealthy man was anxious to make clear to these people the marvelous provision God had made for their salvation. So he caused to be posted in prominent places on his wide domains, notices to the effect that, on a given day, he would be in his office down by the lodge gates, from ten o'clock in the morning until twelve noon. During that time, he would be prepared to pay the debts of all his tenantry who brought their unpaid bills with them.

For days the notices were the cause of much excitement. People talked of the strange offer and some declared it a hoax. Others were certain "there must be a catch somewhere." A few even thought it indicated that the landlord was going out of his mind, for "who had ever heard of any sane man making such an offer?"

When the announced day came, many of the people could be seen making their way to the office, and as the time approached a great crowd had gathered about the door. Promptly at ten the landlord and his secretary drove to the gate, left the carriage and, without a word to anyone, entered the office and closed the door. Outside a great discussion had begun; it became more vehement every minute. Was there anything to it? Did he really mean it? Would he only make a fool of one who brought the evidence of his indebtedness? Some insisted that it was his actual signature at the foot of the notices, and surely he would not dishonor his name. But an hour passed and no one had gone in to present his claim. If one suggested to some one else to venture, he would be met by the angry response, "I don't owe so very much. I have no need to go in. Let some one else try it first—some one who owes more than I do!" And so the precious moments slipped away.

Finally, when it was nearing twelve o'clock, an aged couple from the farthest bounds of the estate came hobbling along arm in arm; the old man had a bundle of bills clutched tightly in one hand. In quavering tones he inquired. "Is it true, neighbor, that the landlord be paying the debts of all who come today?"

"He ain't paid none yet," said one.

"We think it is just a cruel joke," said another.

The old couple's eyes filled with tears. "Is it all a mistake? We hoped it was true and thought how good it would be to be able to die free of debt."

They were turning disconsolately away, when somebody said, "No one has tried him yet. Why not go in? If he pays your bills, come out quickly and tell us and we'll go in, too."

To this the old folks agreed and timidly opened the door and entered the office, where a cordial welcome awaited them. In answer to their question as to whether the notice was true, the secretary said:

"Do you think the landlord would deceive you? Let me see your bills."

They were all presented, carefully tabulated, and a check made out to cover them. Overwhelmed with gratitude, the old man and his wife arose to leave, but the secretary said:

"Just be seated. You must remain here till the office closes at noon."

They explained that the crowd outside was waiting for verification from them of the strange offer.

But the landlord said, "No, you took me at my word. They must do the same if they want their debts paid."

And so the minutes passed. Outside, the people moved restlessly about, watching the closed door, but none lifted the latch. At high noon the door opened and the old folks came out first.

"Did he keep his word?" the throng asked.

"Yes, neighbors. Here is his check and it's good as gold."

"Why didn't you come out and tell us?" angrily asked many.

"He said we must wait inside and you must come as we did and take him at his word."

A moment later the landlord and his secretary came out and hurried to the carriage—the crowd pressing about them, holding out hands full of personal bills, and crying, "Won't you do for us as you did for those folks?" But rising in his carriage, the landlord said, "It is too late now. I gave you every opportunity. I would have paid for you all, but you would not believe me."

Then he likened the events of the morning to the way men treat God's offer to free the sinner of all that divine justice has against him. Solemnly he warned them of the folly of passing up so great salvation until the day of grace was over and it was too late to be saved.

God's Blessed Man

"Blessed is the man that walketh not in the counsel of the ungodly, nor standeth in the way of sinners, nor sitteth in the seat of the scornful" (Psa. 1:1).

I was very much impressed, a number of years ago, as I listened to Joseph Flacks tell of his visit to Palestine. When he was in the city of Jerusalem he was given the opportunity of addressing quite a gathering of Jews and Arabs, all of whom were presumably unconverted. For his text, Mr. Flacks took the first Psalm. Of course, he could repeat it to them in the Hebrew. He dwelt upon the tenses, "Blessed is the man who *hath not* walked in the counsel of the ungodly, nor *stood* in the way of sinners, nor *sat* in the seat of the scornful."

He said to them, "Now, my brethren, who is this blessed man of whom the psalmist speaks? Notice, this happy man is a man who never walked in the counsel of the ungodly, he never stood in the way of sinners, he never sat in the seat of the scornful. He was an absolutely sinless man. Who is this blessed man?" When no one answered, Joseph Flacks said, "Shall we say he is our great Father Abraham? Is it Father Abraham that the psalmist is speaking of here?"

One old Jew said, "No, no, it cannot be Abraham, for he denied his wife; he told a lie about her."

"Ah," said Joseph Flacks, "it does not fit, does it? Abraham, although he was the father of the faithful, yet was a sinner who needed to be justified by faith. But, my brethren, this refers to somebody; who is this man? Could it be our great lawgiver, Moses?"

"No, no," they said, "it cannot be Moses. He killed a man and hid him in the sand." Another added, "And he lost his temper by the water of Meribah."

"Well," Joseph Flacks said, "my brethren, who is it? There is some man here that the Spirit of God is bringing before us. Could it be our great King David, the sweet psalmist of Israel, who perhaps wrote this Psalm?"

"No, no," they cried, "it cannot be David. He committed adultery and had Uriah slain."

"Well," he said, "who is it; to whom do these words refer?"

They were quiet for some little time and then one Jew arose and said, "My brethren, I have a little book here; it is called the New Testament. I have been reading it. If I believed this book, if I could be sure that it is true, I would say that the man of the first Psalm was Jesus of Nazareth."

An old Jew got right up and said, "My brethren, the man of the first Psalm is Jesus of Nazareth. He is the only one who ever went through this world who never walked in the counsel of the ungodly, nor stood in the way of sinners."

Then the old man told how he had been brought to believe in Christ, and he took that occasion to openly confess his faith. He had been searching for a long time and had found out sometime before that Jesus was the One, but he had not had the courage to tell others.

Encouragement To Pray

"And all things, whatsoever ye shall ask in prayer, believing, ye shall receive" (Matt. 21:22).

A number of years ago it was my privilege to attend a Bible conference at which the late Dr. D. M. Stearns was the main speaker. On one particular occasion he had a question hour, and, among the questions there was one that I never forgot. It read something like this: "If you had prayed all your life for the salvation of a loved one, and then you got word that that person had died without giving any evidence of repentance after having lived a sinful life, what would you think, both of prayer itself and of the love of God and His promises to answer?"

It was a very striking question and I know that everyone in the room sat up and wondered what the doctor would have to say in reply to it.

He said, "Well, dear sister, I should expect to meet that loved one in heaven, for I believe in a God who answers prayer, and if He put that exercise upon your heart to pray for that dear one, it was because He, doubtless, intended to answer it."

Then he told a story. Many years ago there was a dear old lady living in Philadelphia who had a very wayward son. This young man had been brought up in church and Sunday school, but he had drifted away from everything holy. He had gone to sea and had become a very rough, careless, godless sailor.

One night his mother was awakened with a very deep sense of need upon her heart. When fully awake, she thought of her son and she was impressed that he was in great danger; as a result^ she got up₃ threw on a dressing gown, knelt by her bedside, and prayed earnestly that God would undertake for the boy, whatever his need was.

She didn't understand it, but after praying for perhaps two or three hours there came to her a sense of rest and peace, and she felt sure in her heart that God had answered. She got back into bed and slept soundly until the morning. Day after day she kept wondering to herself why she was thus awakened and moved to prayer, but somehow or other she could not feel the need to pray for that boy any more; rather she praised God for something which she felt sure He had done for her son.

Several weeks passed. One day there was a knock at the door. When she went to the door—there stood her boy! As soon as he entered the room, he said, "Mother, I'm saved!" Then he told her a wonderful story.

He told how a few weeks earlier, his ship had been tossed in mid-Atlantic by a terrific storm; and it looked as though there were no hope of riding it through. One of the masts had snapped; the captain called the men to come and cut it away. They stepped out, he among them, cursing and reviling God because they had to be out in such an awful night. They were cutting away this mast when suddenly the ship gave a lurch, and a great wave caught this young man and carried him overboard.

As he struggled almost helplessly with the great waves of the sea, the awful thought came to him, "I'm lost forever!" Suddenly, he remembered a hymn that he had often heard sung in his boyhood days, "There is life in a look at the crucified One; There is life at this moment for thee; Then look, sinner, look unto Him and be saved; Unto Him who was nailed to the tree."

He cried out in agony of heart, "Oh, God, I look, I look to Jesus." Then he was carried to the top of the waves and lost consciousness.

Hours afterwards when the storm had ceased and the men came out to clear the deck, they found him lying unconscious, crowded up against a bulwark. Evidently, while one wave had carried him off the deck, another had carried him back again. The sailors took him into the cabin and gave him restoratives. When he came to, the first words from his lips were, "Thank God, I'm saved!" From that time on he had an assurance of God's salvation that meant everything to him.

Then his mother told him how she had prayed for him that night. They realized that it was just at the time when he was in such desperate circumstances, and God had heard and answered.

Now suppose that that young man's body had never been brought back to the ship. Suppose he had sunk down into the depths. People might have thought he was lost forever in his sin, but he would have been as truly saved as he actually was. God had permitted him to come back in testimony of His wonderful grace.

A Negro Preacher On Missions

"I mean not that other men be eased, and ye burdened" (II Cor. 8:13).

We often hear it said by short-sighted Christians that the work at home is likely to suffer if the church pays too much attention to missions and missionary giving. This has been disproved over and over again. A colored preacher was taking an offering for missions, when a close-handed deacon in his congregation called,

"Preacher, you is gwine to kill this church ef you keeps on taking up money for missions."

"Brother," was the reply, "Let me tell you somethin'. Churches don't die that way. An' ef you evah can show me a church what died of giving to missions, I'll go out an' climb upon the ruins of dat church in de light of de moon and preach on de tex' 'Bressed am the dead what dies in de Lawd!'"

The Preacher And Fried Chicken

"Look not every man on his own things, but every man also on the things of others" (Phil. 2:4).

I have never been able to forget a story I heard evangelist Paul Rader relate on one occasion. I may not now be able to recall all the details, but so nearly as I remember, it was as follows:

Mr. Rader mentioned having known three ministers, all of whom came from a particular part of the South and were all characterized by a spirit of intense self-abnegation and kindly interest in the needs of others. To one of these Mr. Rader said, "I have known two other men from your part of the country and you have all commended yourselves to me by your unselfishness. How come that you are all so much alike?"

Modestly the preacher answered, "If we have any such marks as you speak of, we owe our unselfishness to a circuit-rider. When we were just boys he used to come to our section every two weeks."

He then went on to describe him as a lean, cadaverous-looking man of the Abraham Lincoln type who, on the first Sunday he preached in the country schoolhouse, gave a sermon in the morning and another in the afternoon. Between the services the ladies of the congregation served a picnic lunch in the open air. Great platters of fried chicken, ham, and other meats were laid out on gleaming white tablecloths; these were surrounded by stacks of biscuits, corn pone, hard-boiled eggs, cakes and other delicacies. When all was ready, the assembled group sat down on the greensward to enjoy the repast.

A number of lively boys were always at the front, hoping to get nearest to the platter of chicken. But on this particular occasion, so great was the crowd, the boys were told to wait until their elders were all served. Angrily they went off back of a nearby shed and indulged in the pastime of shooting dice, in revenge for the unkind way they felt they had been treated. They appointed one lad as a watcher, to keep tab on the way the viands were disappearing.

Ruefully, he told of piles of chicken disappearing: still, more came in from nearby wagons. Suddenly, in great excitement he exclaimed, "Say, look at that preacher! The old squirrel! He's eaten all he could and now when he thinks no one sees him, he's filling those big pockets in the tail of his long coat." All looked angrily and saw it was indeed true.

Just then one of the women exclaimed, "Why, look at the preacher's plate. You all are neglecting him. Hand over the fried chicken." And she heaped his plate up with appetizing pieces; he nibbled a few minutes—then surreptitiously took two bandana handkerchiefs out of each breast pocket and, filling them with select pieces, stored them away.

Rising with the rest, the preacher backed off, as the boys thought, to hide his "loot" in his baggage. But after moving away from the crowd he turned, and hurried down to the back of the barn where the angry boys were waiting for the second call to lunch. "Boys," he exclaimed, "I was afraid they were forgetting you, so I saved a lot of the white meat and the drumsticks for you." Out came the four clean handkerchiefs and he passed the tender morsels around. The boys were captured. Amazed, they eagerly accepted the proffered dainties.

"This was characteristic of that preacher," said Mr. Rader's friend. "We felt we had found a real friend—a man who loved other people better than he loved himself. He could do anything with us. He led us all to Christ during the years of his ministry among us, sent several out as foreign missionaries, and we three into the ministry at home. It was the unselfish spirit he manifested that gripped our hearts and won our confidence; so that his sermons reached our consciences and brought us to know his Saviour as ours,"

Milk Your Own Cow

"As newborn babes, desire the sincere milk of the word, that ye may grow thereby" (I Pet. 2:2).

Patrick was an Irish Catholic, who for years had longed for the assurance of peace with God. A visiting tourist, who fell into conversation with him, left him a copy of the New Testament, the Douay version, approved by the officials of his church. Through reading this, Pat was brought to a saving knowledge of the Lord Jesus Christ, and from that time on, read and studied his Testament with eagerness, ever seeking a deeper knowledge of the things of God.

The parish priest, who had missed him from the regu- lar services, called on him and found him deep in the study of the Word.

"Pat," he asked, "what is that book you are reading?"

"Sure, your riverence," was the reply, "it's the New Testament."

In horrified accents the priest exclaimed, "The New Testament! Why, Pat, that's not a book for the likes of you. You'll be getting all kinds of wild notions from reading it and will be running off into heresy."

"But, your riverence," remonstrated Pat, "I have just been reading here—it's the blessed apostle Peter himself that wrote it—'As newborn babes, desire the sincere milk of the word, that you may grow thereby,' and sure it's a newborn babe in Christ I am and it's the milk of the Word I'm after. So I can't see the harm of reading the Testament."

"Ah," said the priest, "It's perfectly true, Patrick, that you need the milk of the Word, but the Almighty has appointed the clergy to be the milkmen. The clergy go to the college and the seminary and learn the meaning of the Word and then when the people come to the church we give it to them as they are able to bear it, and explain it in a way that they won't misunderstand."

"Well, sure, your riverence," said Pat, "you know I kape a cow of me own out there in the barn, and when I was sick, sometime ago, I had to hire a man to milk the cow and I soon found he was shtealin' half the milk and fillin' the bucket up with water, and sure it was awful weak milk I was gettin'. But now that I am well again I have let him go and I am milkin' me own cow, and so it's the rich cream I am gettin' once more. And your riverence, when I was dependin' on you for the milk of the Word, sure it was the blue, watery stuff you were givin' me. But now I am milkin' me own cow and enjoyin' the cream of the Word all the time."

We may well emulate Patrick and each for himself milk his own cow and thus get God's Word firsthand as He opens it up by the Holy Spirit.

The Two Natures

"The flesh lusteth against the Spirit, and the Spirit against the flesh: and these are contrary the one to the other" (Gal. 5:17).

An American Indian was giving his testimony in a gathering of Christian members of his tribe. He told of his conversion and of how in the beginning he felt as though he would never sin again; he was so happy in knowing His Saviour. But, he explained, as time went on he became conscious of an inward conflict, which he described somewhat as follows:

"It seems, my brothers, that I have two dogs fighting in my heart: one is a very good dog, a beautiful white dog, and he is always watching out for my best interests. The other is a very bad dog, a black dog, who is always trying to destroy the things that I want to see built up. These dogs give me a lot of trouble because they are always quarreling and fighting with each other."

One of his hearers looked up and asked laconically, "Which one wins?" The other instantly replied, "Whichever one I say 'Sic 'im' to."

Surely there could not be a more apt illustration of the two natures in the believer. "If we walk in the Spirit we shall not fulfil the lusts of the flesh." But if we pander to the flesh, we will be certain to go down in defeat.

Honor To Whom Honor Is Due

"Be not ye called Rabbi" (Matt. 23:8).

"In honor preferring one another" (Rom. 12:10).

On one occasion when in London, I was walking home from a meeting; part of the way I was accompanied by the Marquis of Aberdeen (who had presided) and the Lord Bishop of Norwich (who had been one of the speakers). Being an American, and unaccustomed to titles, I felt embarrassed as to how I should address men of their position. I expressed my perplexity, and the Marquis replied, "My dear brother, just address us as your brethren in Christ. We could have no higher honor than that." This was surely to enter into the spirit of what the Lord Jesus taught.

We are told to give honor to whom honor is due. On the other hand, the servant of Christ is to seek the honor that cometh from God only. The first passage delivers from rudeness and that pride which apes humility, as it refuses to recognize the gifts which Christ has given to His Church. The other is a rebuke to all self-seeking and fleshly ostentation on the part of those to whom the Lord has entrusted any special ministry for the edification of His Church.

Washing Out The Scent

"Some men they follow after" (I Tim. 5:24).

To a Scotsman, the name of Robert, the Bruce, always brings a quickening of the heartstrings as he contemplates the recorded exploits of that heroic personality. I remember well how my young heart was stirred as I read the story of that Scottish chief and liberator, We are told that on one occasion, Bruce was hiding in a mountain glen from King Edward's soldiers. Suddenly he heard the baying of hounds upon the scent, and he recognized them as his own pack which the English had loosed and set upon their master's trail. Though worn with sleepless nights and foodless days, Bruce struggled to his feet and ran as fast as his weary limbs could carry him, with the hounds hot on his track. Nearer and nearer came the sound of baying, and the royal fugitive was almost in despair when he suddenly heard the trickling of a mountain rill. He hastened on and leaped into the stream and down through the waters he sped. Soon he heard the hounds at the brook-side. They were barking excitedly as they ran hither and thither, unable to find the scent. Bruce successfully eluded his enemies because the running water made it impossible for the hounds to follow any further.

Surely this is a picture of the gospel. There is but one way by which any man can escape the judgment of God. That is to plunge into the stream that flows from Calvary's hill, where our blessed Lord made peace by the blood of His Cross. Divine wrath will never reach you there. All sin-stains are washed away and "there is therefore now no condemnation to them which are in Christ Jesus." It was Bruce's own hounds that were tracking him down. Our own sins follow after us, calling for judgment, but the blood of Jesus Christ, God's Son, "cleanseth us from all sin."

Satisfaction In Christ

"I have learned, in whatsoever state I am, therewith to be content" (Phil. 4:11).

Christ is enough to satisfy the hearts of all who confide in Him and who leave everything in His hands. Such need never be cast down by seeming misfortunes.

A Christian asked another how he was getting along. Dolefully his friend replied, "Oh, fairly well, under the circumstances."

"I am sorry," exclaimed the other, "that you are under the circumstances. The Lord would have us living above all circumstances, where He Himself can satisfy our hearts and meet our every need for time and eternity."

On Top Of The Beer Barrel

"What fruit had ye then in those things whereof ye are now ashamed? for the end of those things is death" (Rom. 6:21).

Many years ago, when I was a young Salvation Army officer, it was my privilege to participate in a most unique service at a wide street intersection in the heart of the city of San Diego, California.

We had among our adherents a lovely Christian girl, who was saved out of a very ungodly family. Her father was a saloonkeeper and, while kind to his family and in many respects an admirable character, he had no use for "religion," as he called it, nor for the church. But, through the consistent life of his daughter, he was at last awakened to see his need of a Saviour. He realized that she had something of which he knew nothing, and one night we were all surprised to see him in our audience.

At the close of the service, he came forward, weeping, to confess his sins and seek Christ as his Saviour. We pointed him to the Lord and before the meeting closed, he was rejoicing in the knowledge of sins forgiven.

At once he was faced with the fact that the business in which he was engaged was utterly inconsistent with the Christian life. Some suggested that he should sell out and put the proceeds into some other business. He indignantly spurned the suggestion. Realizing that the saloon was a detriment to humanity, he said he could not, since he had accepted Christ as his Saviour and his Lord, allow himself to profit in any way from the stock of what he afterwards called "liquid damnation." Instead of this, he went to the city authorities and got a permit for what some might have thought was a rather fantastic service.

At the intersection of four streets, near his saloon, he rolled out all the beer barrels and made of them quite a pyramid. The Salvation Army surrounded this rather remarkable spectacle and with band playing and Salvationists singing, soon attracted an immense crowd. The converted saloonkeeper had boxes full of liquor piled up by the pyramid, to the top of which he climbed. "Praise God," he exclaimed as he began his testimony, "I am on top of the beer barrel. For years I used to be under its power, but now I can preach on its head." Then he told, the story of his own conversion and pleaded with sinners to come to his Saviour.

As the liquor bottles were passed up to him, he broke them and spilled their contents over the barrels. Then descending, he set fire to the whole pyramid which went up in a great blaze as the song of the Lord continued. What a remarkable testimony to the power of the gospel of Christ to completely change a life! No longer a saloonkeeper, our friend went into a legitimate business, where his life was a bright testimony to the reality of God's salvation.

"Read Ezekiel 7:8, 9"

"He, that being often reproved hardeneth his neck, shall suddenly be destroyed, and that without remedy" (Prov. 29:1).

The following incident is vouched for by a Church of England clergyman who knew all the circumstances.

A young woman, who had been brought up in a Christian home and who had often had very serious convictions in regard to the importance of coming to Christ, chose instead to take the way of the world. Much against the wishes of her godly mother, she insisted on keeping company with a wild, hilarious crowd, who lived only for the passing moment and tried to forget the things of eternity. Again and again she was pleaded with to turn to Christ, but she persistently refused to heed the admonitions addressed to her.

Finally, she was taken with a very serious illness. All that medical science could do for her was done in order to bring about her recovery, but it soon became evident that the case was hopeless and death was staring her in the face. Still she was hard and obdurate when urged to turn to God in repentance and take the lost sinner's place and trust the lost sinner's Saviour.

One night she awoke suddenly out of a sound sleep, a frightened look in her eyes, and asked excitedly, "Mother, what is Ezekiel 7:8,9?"

Her mother said, "What do you mean, my dear?"

She replied that she had had a most vivid dream. She thought there was a Presence in the room, who very solemnly said to her, "Read Ezekiel 7:8, 9."

Not recalling the verses in question, the mother reached for a Bible. As she opened it, her heart sank as she saw the words, but she read them aloud to the dying girl:

"Now I will shortly pour out my fury upon thee, and accomplish mine anger upon thee: and I will judge thee according to thy ways, and will recompense thee for all thine abominations. And mine eye shall not spare, neither will I have pity: I will recompense thee according to thy ways and thine abominations that are in the midst of thee; and ye shall know that I am the Lord that smiteth."

The poor sufferer, with a look of horror on her face, sank back on the pillow, utterly exhausted, and in a few moments she was in eternity. Once more it had been demonstrated that grace rejected brings judgment at last.

The Lord's Spectacles

"We are made a spectacle ... to angels and to men" (I Cor. 4:9).

One of the colored students of the Southern Bible Training School of Dallas, Texas, was praying and besought the Lord as follows: "O Lord, please keep your spectacles clean so that sinners can see you through us, 'cause you know, Lord, we are your spectacles."

He did not know that the original word "theatron" means a show or display, but supposed it referred to eyeglasses. How we all need to remember that unsaved men can only see Christ through us; and if our lives are unclean, the vision of the Saviour will be blurred!

Accepted In The Beloved

"He hath made us accepted in the beloved" (Eph. 1:6).

Years ago I was preaching in the small town of Roosevelt, Washington, on the north bank of the Columbia River. I was the guest of friends who were sheep-raisers. It was lambing time and every morning we went out to see the lambs—hundreds of them—playing about on the green. One morning I was startled to see an old ewe go loping across the road, followed by the strangest looking lamb I had ever beheld. It apparently had six legs, and the last two were hanging helplessly as though paralyzed, and the skin seemed to be partially torn from its body in a way that made me feel the poor little creature must be suffering terribly. But when one of the herders caught the lamb and brought it over to me, the mystery was explained. That lamb did not really belong originally to that ewe. She had a lamb which was bitten by a rattlesnake and died. This lamb that I saw was an orphan and needed a mother's care. But at first the bereft ewe refused to have anything to do with it. She sniffed at it when it was brought to her, then pushed it away, saying as plainly as a sheep could say it, "That is not our family odor!" So the herders skinned the lamb that had died and very carefully drew the fleece over the living lamb. This left the hind-leg coverings dragging loose. Thus covered, the lamb was brought again to the ewe. She smelled it once more and this time seemed thoroughly satisfied and adopted it as her own.

It seemed to me to be a beautiful picture of the grace of God to sinners. We are all outcasts and have no claim upon His love. But God's own Son, the "Lamb of God, that taketh away the sin of the World," has died for us and now we who believe are dressed up in the fleece of the Lamb who died. Thus, God has accepted us in Him, and "there is therefore now no condemnation to them which are in Christ Jesus." We are as dear to the heart of the Father as His own holy, spotless Son.

"So dear, so very dear to God,

More dear I cannot be;

The love wherewith He loves His Son,

Such is His love to me.

So near, so very near to God,

Nearer I could not be,

For in the person of His Son,

I am as near as He."

Standing Where The Fire Has Been

"Who loved me and gave himself for me" (Gal. 2:20).

One of the first gospel illustrations that ever made a real impression upon my young heart was a simple story which I heard a preacher tell when I was less than nine years old.

It was of pioneers who were making their way across one of the central states to a distant place that had been opened up for homesteading. They traveled in covered wagons drawn by oxen, and progress was necessarily slow. One day they were horrified to note a long line of smoke in the west, stretching for miles across the prairie, and soon it was evident that the dried grass was burning fiercely and coming toward them rapidly. They had crossed a river the day before but it would be impossible to go back to that before the flames would be upon them. One man only seemed to have understanding as to what should be done. He gave the command to set fire to the grass behind them. Then when a space was burned over, the whole company moved back upon it.

As the flames roared on toward them from the west, a little girl cried out in terror, "Are you sure we shall not all be burned up?" The leader replied, "My child, the flames cannot reach us here, for we are standing where the fire has been!"

What a picture of the believer, who is safe in Christ!

"On Him Almighty vengeance fell,

Which would have sunk a world to hell.

He bore it for a chosen race,

And thus becomes our Hiding Place."

The fires of God's judgment burned themselves out on Him, and all who are in Christ are safe forever, for they are now standing where the fire has been.

A Victim Of Wrong Information

"Though we, or an angel from heaven, preach any other gospel unto .... let him be accursed" (Gal. 1:8).

I remember reading a story of a woman who with her little babe was travelling by train through one of the northeastern states. It was a very wintry day. Outside a terrific storm was blowing, snow was falling, and sleet covered everything. The train made its way along slowly because of the ice on the tracks and the snowplow went ahead to clear the way. The woman seemed very nervous. She was to get off at a small station, where she would be met by some friends, and she said to the conductor, "You will be sure and let me know the right station, won't you?"

"Certainly," he said, "just remain here until I tell you the right station."

She sat rather nervously, and again spoke to the conductor, "You won't forget me?"

"No, just trust me. I will tell you when to get off."

A commercial man sat across the aisle. He leaned over and said, "Pardon me, but I see you are rather nervous about getting off at your station. I know this road well. Your station is the first stop after such and such a city. These conductors are very forgetful, they have a great many things to attend to, and he may overlook your request, but I will see that you get off all right. I will help you with your baggage."

"Oh, thank you," she said. And she leaned back greatly relieved.

By and by the brakeman called the name of the city the commercial traveler had mentioned, and the latter said to the woman, "Yours is the next station. Better get ready and I will assist you to get off."

The train moved on and shortly afterwards came to a full stop. The woman hurried to the end of the car, the man who was helping her carrying her bag. When they reached the vestibule, there was no one there. "You see," said the stranger, "these trainmen are very careless. The conductor has quite forgotten you." But he opened the door, assisted the woman with her baby down the steps, and just as he boarded the train again it moved on.

A few minutes later the conductor came through the train and looking all about, said, "Why, that is strange! There was a woman here who wanted to get off at the next station, I wonder where she is."

The commercial man spoke up and said, "Yes, you forgot her, but I saw that she got off all right."

"Got off where?" the conductor asked.

"When the train stopped."

"But that was not a station! That was an emergency stop! I was looking after that woman. Why, man, you have put her off in a wild country district in the midst of all this storm, where there will be nobody to meet her!"

There was only one thing to do, and, although it was a rather dangerous thing, they had to reverse the engine and go back a number of miles, and then went out to look for the woman. They searched and searched; finally, somebody stumbled upon her body. She was frozen on the ground, her little babe dead in her arms. She was the victim of wrong information.

If it is such a serious thing to give people wrong information in regard to temporal things, what about the man who misleads men and women in regard to the great question of the salvation of their immortal souls? If men believe a false gospel, if they put their trust in something that is contrary to the Word of God, their loss will be not for time only, but for eternity,

Cobbling For The Glory Of God

"Do all in the name of the Lord Jesus" (Col. 3:17).

When I was a boy, I felt it was both a duty and a privilege to help my widowed mother make ends meet by finding employment in vacation time, on Saturdays and other times when I did not have to be in school. For quite a while I worked for a Scottish shoemaker, or "cobbler," as he preferred to be called, an Orkney man, named Dan Mackay. He was a forthright Christian and his little shop was a real testimony for Christ in the neighborhood. The walls were literally covered with Bible texts and pictures, generally taken from old-fashioned Scripture Sheet Almanacs, so that look where one would, he found the Word of God staring him in the face. There were John 3:16 and John 5:24, Romans 10:9, and many more.

On the little counter in front of the bench on which the owner of the shop sat, was a Bible, generally open, and a pile of gospel tracts. No package went out of that shop without a printed message wrapped inside. And whenever opportunity offered, the customers were spoken to kindly and tactfully about the importance of being born again and the blessedness of knowing that the soul is saved through faith in Christ. Many came back to ask for more literature or to inquire more particularly as to how they might find peace with God, with the blessed results that men and women were saved, frequently right in the shoe-shop.

It was my chief responsibility to pound leather for shoe soles. A piece of cowhide would be cut to suit, then soaked in water. I had a flat piece of iron over my knees and, with a flat-headed hammer, I pounded these soles until they were hard and dry. It seemed an endless operation to me, and I wearied of it many times.

What made my task worse was the fact that, a block away, there was another shop that I passed going and coming to or from my home, and in it sat a jolly, godless cobbler who gathered the boys of the neighborhood about him and regaled them with lewd tales that made him dreaded by respectable parents as a menace to the community. Yet, somehow, he seemed to thrive and that perhaps to a greater extent than my employer, Mackay. As I looked in his window, I often noticed that he never pounded the soles at all, but took them from the water, nailed them on, damp as they were, and with the water splashing from them as he drove each nail in.

One day I ventured inside, something I had been warned never to do. Timidly, I said, "I notice you put the soles on while still wet. Are they just as good as if they were pounded?" He gave me a wicked leer as he answered, "They come back all the quicker this way, my boy!"

Feeling I had learned something, I related the instance to my boss and suggested that I was perhaps wasting time in drying out the leather so carefully. Mr. Mackay stopped his work and opened his Bible to the passage that reads, "Whatsoever ye do, do all to the glory of God."

"Harry," he said, "I do not cobble shoes just for the four bits or six bits (50c or 75c) that I get from my customers.

I am doing this for the glory of God. I expect to see every shoe I have ever repaired in a big pile at the judgment seat of Christ, and I do not want the Lord to say to me in that day, 'Dan, this was a poor job. You did not do your best here.' I want Him to be able to say, 'Well done, good and faithful servant.'"

Then he went on to explain that just as some men are called to preach, so he was called to fix shoes, and that only as he did this well would his testimony count for God. It was a lesson I have never been able to forget. Often when I have been tempted to carelessness, and to slipshod effort, I have thought of dear, devoted Dan Mackay, and it has stirred me up to seek to do all as for Him who died to redeem me.

Blind Leaders Of The Blind

"If the blind lead the blind, both shall fall into the ditch" (Matt. 15:14).

On one occasion Col. Robert G. Ingersoll, the agnostic lecturer of the last century, was announced to give an address on hell. He declared he would prove conclusively that hell was a wild dream of some scheming theologians who invented it to terrify credulous people. As he was launching into his subject, a half-drunken man arose in the audience and exclaimed, "Make it strong, Bob. There's a lot of us poor fellows depending on you. If you are wrong, we are all lost. So be sure you prove it clear and plain." No amount of reasoning can nullify God's sure Word. He has spoken as plainly of a hell for the finally impenitent as of a heaven for those who are saved.

Law And Grace

"We are not under the law, but under grace" (Rom. 6:15).

Some years ago, I had a little school for young Indian men and women, who came to my home in Oakland, California, from the various tribes in northern Arizona. One of these was a Navajo young man of unusually keen intelligence. One Sunday evening, he went with me to our young people's meeting. They were talking about the epistle to the Galatians, and the special subject was law and grace. They were not very clear about it, and finally one turned to the Indian and said, "I wonder whether our Indian friend has anything to say about this."

He rose to his feet and said, "Well, my friends, I have been listening very carefully, because I am here to learn all I can in order to take it back to my people. 1 do not understand all that you are talking about, and I do not think you do yourselves. But concerning this law and grace business, let me see if I can make it clear. I think it is like this. When Mr. Ironside brought me from my home we took the longest railroad journey I ever took. We got out at Barstow, and there I saw the most beautiful railroad station and hotel I have ever seen. I walked all around and saw at one end a sign, 'Do not spit here.' I looked at that sign and then looked down at the ground and saw many had spitted there, and before I think what I am doing I have spitted myself. Isn't that strange when the sign say, 'Do not spit here'?

"I come to Oakland and go to the home of the lady who invited me to dinner today and I am in the nicest home I have ever been in. Such beautiful furniture and carpets, I hate to step on them. I sank into a comfortable chair, and the lady said, 'Now, John, you sit there while I go out and see whether the maid has dinner ready.' I look around at the beautiful pictures, at the grand piano, and I walk all around those rooms. I am looking for a sign; the sign I am looking for is, 'Do not spit here,' but I look around those two beautiful drawing rooms, and cannot find a sign like this. I think, 'What a pity when this is such a beautiful home to have people spitting all over it—too bad they don't put up a sign!' So I look all over that carpet, but cannot find that anybody have spitted there. What a queer thing! Where the sign says, 'Do not spit,' a lot of people spitted. Where there was no sign at all, in that beautiful home, nobody spitted. Now I understand! That sign is law, but inside the home it is grace. They love their beautiful home, and they want to keep it clean. They do not need a sign to tell them so. I think that explains the law and grace business."

As he sat down, a murmur of approval went round the room and the leader exclaimed, "I think that is the best illustration of law and grace I have ever heard."

The Gift Of God

"The gift of God is eternal life through Jesus Christ, our Lord" (Rom. 6:23).

You cannot earn a gift. It would cease to be a gift if it were purchased with money, or paid for, in whole or in part, in any other way.

Years ago, a wealthy lady in New York built a beautiful church. On the day of dedication her agent came up from the audience to the platform and handed the deed of the property to the Episcopal Bishop of New York. The bishop gave the agent $1.00 for the deed, and by virtue of the $1.00, which was acknowledged, the property was turned over to the Episcopal Church.

You say, "What a wonderful gift!" Yes, in a certain sense it was, for the passing over of $1.00 was simply a legal observance. But after all, in the full Bible sense it was not a gift, for it cost $1.00; and so the deed was made out, not as a deed of gift, but as a deed of sale. It was sold to the Episcopal Church for $1.00.

If you had to do one thing in order to be saved, if you had even to raise your hand, to stand to your feet, had but to say one word, it would not be a gift. You could say, "I did thus and so, and in that way earned my salvation." But this priceless blessing is absolutely free.

"If by grace, then is it no more of works: otherwise grace is no more grace. But if it be of works, then is it no more grace: otherwise work is no more work" (Rom. 11:6). That is what the Spirit of God tells us in the Word.

The New Man

"Whosoever is born of God doth not commit (that is, practice) sin; for his seed remaineth in him and he cannot sin, because he is born of God" (I John 3:9).

It is the grace of God working in the soul that makes the believer delight in holiness, in righteousness, in obedience to the will of God, for real joy is found in the service of the Lord Jesus Christ. I remember a man who lived a life of gross sin.

After his conversion, one of his old friends said to him, "Bill, I pity you—a man that has been such a high-flier as you. And now you have settled down; you go to church, or stay at home and read the Bible and pray; you never have good times any more."

"But, Bob," said the man, "you don't understand. I get drunk every time I want to. I go to the theater every time I want to. I go to the dance when I want to. I play cards and gamble whenever I want to."

"I say, Bill," said his friend, "I didn't understand it that way. I thought you had to give up these things to be a Christian."

"No, Bob," said Bill, "the Lord took the 'want to' out when He saved my soul, and He made me a new creature in Christ Jesus."

When we are born of God we receive a new life and that life has its own new nature, a nature that hates sin and impurity and delights in holiness and goodness.

The Wrong Remedy

"They have healed the hurt of the daughter of my people slightly, saying, Peace, peace; when there is no peace" (Jer. 8:11).

When I was a boy, I heard a North of Ireland preacher relate the following story, which he declared to be absolutely authentic. It is a striking illustration of the lack of understanding of spiritual problems prevalent in some quarters, even in our enlightened days. In a Scottish home the younger son, a lad in his late teens, named Robert, (generally "Robbie" in the family) became troubled about his soul. Realizing he was a lost sinner, he sought in vain for some one who could make plain to him the way of peace with God. His father, though a religious man and an esteemed office-bearer in the local kirk, could not understand why a lad brought up as his son had been should think himself lost and in need of salvation.

In his distress the boy sought out the minister, who after a long talk with him told him he should put away such gloomy thoughts and try to get his mind on brighter things. As the youth was musically inclined, the pastor suggested to the father to purchase a fiddle for his son and have him take violin lessons. This was done, but although Robbie tried to forget his "gloomy ideas" (as the minister called them) and resolutely set himself to learn to play the fiddle, he at last gave up in despair. "I cannot fiddle," he exclaimed, "when I am lost in my sins and may die any moment and go into hell because I cannot find how to be saved."

A physician was called in, who, after examining the boy, advised that he be sent to a sanitarium for mental cases, as he felt sure he was losing his mind, and if not properly treated, might do something desperate.

So to the asylum the poor lad was taken. There for weeks he paced a narrow room in anguish of soul, as he exclaimed again and again, "Oh, that I knew how to get rid o' my sins!"

One day, a lady who knew Christ came to that institution in order to help and comfort a friend of hers who had suffered a nervous breakdown. As she passed the room of poor Robbie she heard his sobs and wondered if it was a case of conviction of sin rather than incipient insanity. She was given an opportunity to speak with him and, after hearing his story, she pointed him to Christ and left with him a New Testament, marking several passages, which she asked him to read carefully. As he pondered these verses, telling of Christ's finished work and the blood that cleanseth from all sin, light from heaven shone into his darkened soul and soon he was rejoicing in God's salvation.

The change in his behavior was so notable that the attending alienist decided he was cured by the treatment received, and he notified the father that Robbie might now safely be taken home. His brother James came for him and was delighted to find Robbie so calm and peaceful. Little was said until he arrived at home, when, in response to his anxious father's question, "Are ye a' right noo, Robbie?" he exclaimed, "Aye, feyther, I'm a'right noo, for my sins are gone an' my soul is saved!" The shocked father cried out aghast, "Jamie, gang for the meenister. Tell him Robbie's had a relapse, and to come at once."

When the minister reached the house, Robbie greeted him somewhat sternly, "Meenister, Meenister," he exclaimed, "why did ye set me trying to fiddle my sins awa'? Why did ye no tell me o' the bluid o' Jesus that cleanses frae a' sin. What the fiddlin could na' do, the Lord Jesus has done for me."

The embarrassed minister soon realized a work of God had taken place in the soul of the young man. Though he did not fathom it all, he understood enough to know it was what the Bible calls being "born again," and so he assured the father he need not worry about his son's mentality. As the time went on, all knew that Robbie had indeed passed from death unto life and many were won to Christ through his testimony.

It is to be feared there are many in our days who are as unable to help a troubled soul as was Robbie's pastor. Yet every one who professes to be a minister of God should be an expert at dealing with anxious men and women and showing them the only way of life and peace—through the gospel of His grace.

A Lost Opportunity

"As thy servant was busy here and there, he was gone" (I Kings 20:40).

Ambassador Wu Ting Fang was one of the most colorful oriental diplomats ever accredited to Washington. He came as the representative of the Chinese Empire and for several years occupied that post in this country. When he was recalled to China, it was announced that he would leave for his native land from New York City at a given, date. Noticing that he would be in the metropolis over the Lord's Day, the pastor of the Chinese Church on the East Side sent him a polite letter inviting him to attend one of their services on that occasion.

The ambassador replied at once. In his letter he told how, when he first came to America, he had been intensely interested in the Christian religion, as he felt that it was in some very definite way the real source of the enlightened civilization of this great country. He said he then and there made up his mind that he would never refuse an invitation to attend a Christian service, if it were at all possible for him to accept. "I have been in this country six years," he wrote, "and yours is the first such invitation I have ever received!"

What a tragic commentary on the indifference of Christians to the need of those who are strangers to the gospel! Who can weigh aright the guilt of Christians who were acquainted with this great statesman and never once attempted to win him for Christ? Let us all remember the admonition, "Redeeming the time (buying up opportunities) for the days are evil."

Example Of New Birth

"Of his own will begat he us with the word of truth" (Jas. 1:18).

The folly of supposing that anyone can be saved by the power of a great example comes out clearly in an incident related on one occasion by Dr. Joseph Parker, then pastor of the City Temple, London, England.

Paderewski, the great Polish pianist, had given a concert that day in the city, and at night, addressing a large congregation, Dr. Parker spoke somewhat as follows:

"I have had today most forcibly presented to me the folly of trusting in the power of a great example. Many of you know that I have always been a lover of music and some of my friends have been kind enough to try to make me believe that I had some talent as a pianist. It has often been my delight, when weary of other things, to sit down at my piano and play some of the classical selections, or improvise, according to my mood.

"But today a friend took me to hear that great master of the piano—Paderewski. For two hours I sat enthralled, listening to music such as I had never heard in all my life before. When the last lovely note was struck and the applause had died away, I felt I wanted to slip out quietly, speaking to no one, with the thrill of it still stirring my soul.

"An hour or so later, I was standing before my piano, when I was summoned for dinner. At first I did not hear the summons and when my wife came to me, I turned to her and said, almost savagely, I am afraid, 'Bring me an ax.'

"She looked at me anxiously and asked, 'My dear, what do you mean?'

"I said, 'You know I have always thought I was something of a pianist, but I have heard real music today for the first time and I realize now that what I thought was musical talent amounts to nothing. I feel like chopping my piano all to pieces. I never want to touch it again.'

"That was the effect of a great example upon my mind. I know that I shall overcome this and I shall soon enjoy my piano as I did in the past, but I realized then, and I realize now, that no example, such as that of Paderewski, could ever make a great musician of me. In order to play as he played, one must have the soul of a Paderewski. To try to imitate him would be folly. And so it is in regard to the matter of our salvation. It is true that Christ has left us an example that we should follow His steps, but before we can do that, we need to receive the Spirit of Christ—we must be born again. There must be the very life of Christ communicated to us."

Dr. Parker was right. No one can ever be saved by attempting to follow Christ's example. It is absolutely fundamental that we first be born again.

An Arrow Shot At A Venture

"Ye must be born again" (John 3:7).

When Bishop John Taylor Smith, former Chaplain General of the British Army, was in this country at the time of the D. L. Moody Centenary meetings, it was my privilege to hear him one noon hour in Christ Church,

Indianapolis. The sanctuary was crowded with eager listeners, to whom the Bishop spoke most solemnly, yet tenderly, upon the necessity of the new birth, using the text quoted above. As a telling illustration, he related the following incident:

On one occasion, he told us, he was preaching in a large cathedral on this same text. In order to drive it home, he said: "My dear people, do not substitute anything for the new birth. You may be a member of a church, even the great church of which I am a member, the historic Church of England, but church membership is not new birth, and 'except a man be born again he cannot see the kingdom of God.' The rector was sitting at my left. Pointing to him, I said, You might be a clergyman like my friend the rector here and not be born again, and 'except a man be born again he cannot see the kingdom of God.' On my left sat the archdeacon in his stall. Pointing directly at him, I said, You might even be an archdeacon like my friend in his stall and not be born again and 'except a man be born again he cannot see the kingdom of God.' You might even be a bishop, like myself, and not be born again and 'except a man be born again he cannot see the kingdom of God.'"

Then he went on to tell us that a day or so later he received a letter from the archdeacon, in which he wrote: "My dear Bishop: You have found me out. I have been a clergyman for over thirty years, but I had never known anything of the joy that Christians speak of. I never could understand it. Mine has been hard, legal service. I did not know what was the matter with me, but when you pointed directly to me and said, You might even be an archdeacon and not be born again, I realized in a moment what the trouble was. I had never known anything of the new birth."

He went on to say that he was wretched and miserable, had been unable to sleep all night, and begged for a conference, if the bishop could spare the time to talk with him.

"Of course, I could spare the time," said Bishop Smith, "and the next day we got together over the Word of God and after some hours we were both on our knees, the archdeacon taking his place before God as a poor, lost sinner and telling the Lord Jesus he would trust Him as his Saviour. From that time on everything has been different."

It was a striking example of the absolute necessity of birth from above, and of the sad possibility of being deceived with a false profession and going on for years not understanding one's true condition before God.

Possessing Our Possessions

"He that ... believeth ... hath everlasting life" (John 5:24).

Believing God's testimony is like endorsing a check and cashing it. A gentleman went into the home of a very poor old lady who had applied for relief. He saw something on the wall that attracted his attention. It was a piece of paper in a neat frame.

He asked, "What is that on the wall?"

She replied, "I just don't know what it is, but it is a paper my uncle sent me and I just don't like to throw it away and so I keep it there in remembrance of him."

He exclaimed, "Don't you see what it is!"

"No, I just don't understand it."

"Well, it's a bank check. Look! There is the name of the bank on which it is drawn and it says, 'Pay to Jennie Johnson the sum of $5,000.00' and there is your uncle's name at the bottom of it."

"What," she said, "did he intend me to have that money? and I have been living in poverty all these years!"

How many people are like that. They believe the Word and God's promises—in a certain sense. They know Jesus died to put away sin. But they have never cashed in, they have never trusted Him for themselves.

The Cleansing Word

"That he might sanctify and cleanse it with the washing of water by the word" (Eph. 5:26).

The Word is for cleansing as well as for instruction, and if it keeps going through you it will have a marvelous effect upon your mind and heart and life. It will cleanse and purify you and fit you to be a real worker for the Lord Jesus Christ.

You remember the story of the Scotch laddie who was one of those pernickety youngsters who always wanted a reason for everything he was told to do. He was working for a farmer and when the old man told him to do anything, the lad generally asked, "Why?" This disturbed his employer.

On one occasion he said to the boy as he handed him a market basket, "Take this basket down to the creek and fill it with water." When the laddie asked, "Why?" and started to explain that it would not hold water, the old man replied, "None o' yer 'whys.' I'm paying for your time; you do as I tell you."

So the boy started for the creek with the basket in his hand. Wading into the water, he dipped the basket into the creek and lifted it up. Of course, the water all ran out.

Disgusted, he said, "It will no' hold the water."

The old farmer replied, "Fill it up again."

Again the lad obeyed, and once more the water all ran through.

His master said, "Fill it again."

This time the boy answered, "I'll fill it up once more, but if it does no' hold this time, you will no make me a fool again."

So he dipped it into the creek the third time, but as he held it up, the water all ran out. Angry, he flung the basket over into the grass, saying, "Take your auld kreel; I'll no be a fool fer ye or anybody else."

The old man picked it up good naturedly and then held it between him and the sun. As he examined it carefully, he explained, "It's a guid deal cleaner than it was, and that's what it needed." The water running through it had cleansed away the dirt, and this is how the Word of God affects our lives.

Our Lord Jesus prayed, "Sanctify them through thy truth; thy word is truth." We are sanctified by the washing of the water by the Word. We cannot give too much time to the study of this blessed Book. I do not mean merely studying it in order to get sermons out of it, but what we need is a daily, thoughtful, prayerful study of the Word for the nourishment of our own souls, for building ourselves up in our most holy faith,

In The Cleft Of The Rock

"Call upon me in the day of trouble: I will deliver thee" (Psa. 50:15).

Years ago, while working among the Laguna Indians, we were asked to speak at a little village called Pawate. It was in the days before automobiles, and we rode in large wagons drawn by horses for some fourteen miles over rough roads until we reached this village. We had a meeting in the afternoon, and Indians from all about gathered. We started back at 4:30 or 5 o'clock because we were to have a meeting at Casa Blanca that night. We had not gone very far when we saw a terrible storm was about to break over us. Soon we could see that the rain was pouring down at a distance and driving rapidly toward us.

I said, "We are certainly going to get soaked."

Our driver replied, "I hope not. I think we can make the rock before the storm reaches us. There is a great rock ahead; and if we can make it, we will be sheltered."

We hurried on and soon saw a vast rock rising right up from the plain, perhaps forty or fifty feet in height, covering possibly an acre or more of ground. As we drew near, we saw a great cave in the rock. Instead of stopping to unhitch the horses, our driver drove right into the cave, and, in another minute or two, the storm broke over the rock in all its fury.

While the storm raged outside, one of the Indians struck up, in the Laguna tongue, "Rock of Ages, cleft for me, let me hide myself in Thee," and we realized the meaning of the poet's words then as perhaps never before.

A Butterfly Used To Answer Prayer

"Is there anything too hard for me?" (Jer. 32:27).

An English evangelist, whom I have learned to know and love, Mr. H. P. Barker, tells an interesting story of a poor woman who was being pressed by a tradesman to pay an account which she knew she had already settled. In that case he demanded that she produce a receipt; quite certain she had received one she hunted and hunted, but was absolutely unable to find it. She went through piles of. papers and letters, but to no avail—the receipt was not forthcoming. Finally the tradesman came to her again and made a very angry demand upon her for immediate payment.

In her distress she turned to the Lord in earnest prayer, asking Him to bring the receipt to light. Then in a moment or two, a butterfly flew into the room through an open window, and her little boy, eager to catch the beautiful creature, ran after it. The frightened insect flew over to the wall on one side and down behind a trunk. The boy in his eagerness to catch it, pushed out the trunk, and there, behind it on the floor lay the missing receipt! Snatching it up triumphantly, the poor widow showed it to the tradesman, who went away discomfited. As his own handwriting declared, the debt had been paid.

Who can doubt but that He who notes the sparrow's fall and who would have us learn lessons from the ant and the coney and other small creatures, directed even the movements of a butterfly in order that He might answer His handmaiden's prayer!

Only Three Weeks To Live

"He that believeth .... is not condemned" (John 3:18).

A number of years ago I was holding special meetings in the First Baptist Church of Los Gatos, California. On my first Sunday morning there, the text was: "Whosoever drinketh of this water shall thirst again: but whosoever drinketh of the water that I shall give him shall never thirst; but the water that I shall give him shall be in him a well of water springing up into everlasting life" (John 4:13, 14). Sitting in the front pew was a young woman whose pale emaciated face and great, dark, hungry eyes attracted my attention. She listened so earnestly.

After the meeting I said to the pastor: "Who was the very sickly but intensely beautiful girl who sat in the front pew?"

"She is a very well bred girl," he replied, "but some years ago she threw Christianity to the winds. She was brought up in a Christian home. She went in for a worldly career, trying to find satisfaction and peace in the things of the world, but, within the last five months, she has been stricken with that dread disease of tuberculosis, and she has the kind that we call galloping consumption. She has not long to live; she is losing strength day after day, and the doctor says she will soon be gone; and now she is wretched and miserably unhappy."

I prayed for her, and each night I would find myself looking through that audience, hoping she would be there, listening to the gospel, but I never saw her at another meeting.

About three weeks later a lady came to me and said: "Do you remember meeting Miss H—?" I remembered that it was this young lady, and she added, "She is very ill, dying of tuberculosis. She heard you the first time you spoke, and was expecting to attend all the meetings, but she has been too ill. She has sent for you."

"I will be glad to go," was my reply. So we went to the room in which she sat. She excused herself for not standing to greet us, for she was too weak. I said, "I am glad that you have sent for me."

She looked up and said, "Mr. Ironside, the doctor told me yesterday that I have just three weeks to live, and I am not saved. I would like to know Christ. Do you think He will take a girl who rejected Him, deliberately turned her back on Him in health, now that I am bitterly disappointed, and everything I have counted on has gone by the board? Do you think there is any hope for a sinner like me?"

You know things look different when you realize you have only three weeks to live! Many a one, careless now, would be in dead earnest if he knew that within three weeks he would have to face God and eternity.

"Well," I said, "I understand that you have had a very happy life in some respects; you have been very much sought after and admired by the world."

"Oh, please do not talk of that now," she said, "I am afraid I have been selling my soul for worldly popularity. I thought I was going to find happiness and enjoyment, but now it gives me no peace, no satisfaction, to look back over those years of popularity, those years of worldly pleasure. Only three weeks and I must give an account to God, and I am not saved."

It was a real joy to my own soul to open the Word of God and show her how the blessed Lord Jesus in infinite grace had come all the way from heaven's fullest glory down to Calvary's deepest depths of woe for her redemption, and if she would put her heart trust in Him and confess her guilt, she would have all the past blotted out Directing her to John 3:18, I read: "He that believeth on him is not condemned: but he that believeth not is condemned already, because he hath not believed in the name of the only begotten Son of God." And then I put the question to her, "Tell me, do you believe the Lord Jesus Christ is the Son of God?" "I do."

Then I asked her, "Do you believe that God the Father sent Him into this world to die for sinners?"

"Yes, it is in the Bible: I do believe it," she replied. "Do you believe He meant you when He said: 'Him that cometh unto me I will in no wise cast out?'" I asked. "It is for everybody, isn't it," she said. "Yes," I replied, "'For God so loved the world, that he gave his only begotten Son, that whosoever believeth in him should not perish, but have everlasting life' (John 3:16). Are you included in that whosoever?" "Yes," she said, "I believe I am."

"Then tell me," I said, "what does the Lord Jesus Christ say about you? Look at verse eighteen again; notice there are only two classes of people there: the first class, 'He that believeth on him,' and the second class, 'He that believeth not.' Notice that there is something predicated of the first class and something of the second class. Of the first it is said, 'He that believeth is not condemned'; and of the second, 'He that believeth not is condemned already.' Now before I ask you to tell me which class you are in, let us bow in prayer."

She could not kneel, but her friend and I knelt in prayer. We asked God by the Spirit to open His Word and bring it home in power to her soul.

"Read it again," I said.

"Do you see the two classes? Which one are you in?"

She was silent for a long time as we knelt there before God, and then she looked up, the tears glistening in her beautiful eyes, and she said, "I am in the first class."

"How do you know?"

"Because I do believe in Him. It doesn't say He won't take me in because I come so late. I have come, and I do believe in Him."

"And what is true of you?" I asked.

She looked at it again and whispered, "Not condemned!"

I said, "Is that enough to meet God on?"

She replied, "That will do; not condemned!"

Three weeks from eternity, but resting upon the Word of God! I saw her only twice again, and then my meetings ended. About five weeks later I met the Baptist preacher on the street, and he said, "You remember Miss H—? Do you know that just twenty-one days from the day you led her to Christ, I was called *o her bedside, and I found her just slipping away? 'Can you hear me?' I asked. 'Yes,' she said. 'Do you believe on the Lord Jesus Christ?' 'Yes,' she answered. 'And what does He say about you?' I asked.

'Not condemned!' and then she whispered, 'If you see Mr. Ironside, tell him it is all right.'"

Oh, I tell you, dear friend, that was something real, because that young woman had the Word of the living God to rest upon; but there are many who rest upon their own imaginations instead of renting on God's immutable Word.

Patriotism-Plus

"Greater love hath no man than this, that a man lay down his life for his friends" (John 15:13).

"When we were enemies, we were reconciled to God by the death of his Son" (Rom. 5:10).

When nations are engaged in deadly strife, it is common for patriots to declare that he who gives his life for defence of his country may be certain of a home in heaven because of having made the supreme sacrifice. This teaching is in accord with the principles of the Moslem religion and not with true Christianity. Mahomet promised his fanatical followers a place in Paradise if they died for the faith in conflict with the "infidels" who rejected his teachings. Patriotism is a virtue of which any man may well be proud.

"Lives there a man with soul so dead, Who never to himself hath said, This is my own, my native land?" But patriotism, praiseworthy as it is from a human standpoint, will never fit the soul for the presence of God. It can never wash away the guilt of sin.

The testimony of Edith Cavell, the brave British nurse who was killed by the Germans during the former world war, is well worth considering in this connection.

This noble woman was born at Swardeston, Norfolk, on December 4, 1865. She entered the London Hospital for nurses' training in 1895. In 1907 she was appointed first matron of the Berkendael Medical Institute at Brussels, Belgium. This became the Red Cross Hospital for Belgium at the outbreak of the conflict in 1914. From August of that year, until August, 1915, Nurse Cavell helped to care for wounded French, Belgian, English and German soldiers alike. She ministered faithfully even to those who had fallen while fighting against her own nation. Naturally, her sympathies were with the Allies, and in cooperation with the efforts of Prince Reginald de Croy, she aided many derelict English and French soldiers who had fled from the Germans. These escaped by "underground" methods to the Dutch frontier, where, with the aid of guides, they were conveyed across to Britain. When some of these fugitives were traced to her house in Brussels, she was immediately arrested and after a court-martial was sentenced to face a firing-squad. All her kindness to the German wounded was forgotten. Her captors considered her a spy and treated her accordingly.

Just before the bandage was placed over her eyes, as she stood fearlessly facing the soldiers who were about to take her life, she gave a last message to the world. "I am glad," she said, "to die for my country. But as I stand here I realize as never before that *patriotism is not enough.*" Then she went on to give a clear, definite testimony to her personal faith in the Lord Jesus Christ and her assurance of salvation, not through laying down her life for others, but because He laid down His life for her. In perfect composure, she submitted to the bandaging of her eyes and, in a few moments fell, pierced by many German bullets.

Her words, *patriotism is not enough!* have spoken loudly to many in the years that have gone since she died a martyr to her convictions. Yet many forget this.

"What more *is* needed?" you may ask. The answer is "Christ!" It is through faith in Him alone that the soul is saved and heaven assured.

Why The Train Was Wrecked

"It is the blood that maketh an atonement for the soul" (Lev. 17:11).

Some years ago a fearful railroad wreck took a dreadful toll of life and limb in an eastern state. A train, loaded with young people returning from school, was stalled on a suburban track because of what is known as a "hot-box." The limited was soon due, but a flagman was sent back to warn the engineer in order to avert a rear-end collision. Thinking all was well, the crowd laughed and chatted while the train-hands worked on in fancied security. Suddenly the whistle of the limited was heard and on came the heavy train and crashed into the local, with horrible effect.

The engineer of the limited saved his own life by jumping, and some days afterwards was hailed into court to account for his part in the calamity. And now a curious discrepancy in testimony occurred. He was asked, "Did you not see the flagman warning you to stop?"

He replied, "I saw him, but he waved a yellow flag, and I took it for granted all was well, and so went on, though slowing down."

The flagman was called, "What flag did you wave?"

"A red flag, but he went by me like a shot."

"Are you sure it was red?"

"Absolutely."

Both insisted on the correctness of their testimony, and it was demonstrated that neither was color-blind. Finally the man was asked to produce the flag itself as evidence. After some delay he was able to do so, and then the mystery was explained, *It had been red,* but it had been exposed to the weather so long that all the red was bleached out, and it was but *a dirty yellow!*

Oh, the lives eternally wrecked by the yellow gospels of the day—the bloodless theories of unregenerate men that send their hearers to their doom instead of stopping them on their downward road!

The Hen And The Lizard

"Look not thou upon the wine when it is red, when it giveth his color in the cup, when it moveth itself aright. At the last it biteth like a serpent, and stingeth like an adder" (Prov. 23:31, 32).

Sometime ago, a friend of mine, an evangelist, and his wife, living in Southern California, were watching a flock of chickens at feeding time, when they noticed one hen that seemed to be attempting to swallow a large lizard. She was fluttering wildly about and a lot of the other hens were cackling loudly as they gathered about her. Going over to see what was taking place, they found that while the hen had evidently pecked at the lizard, the slimy, twisting creature had turned about and had the hen by the throat and would have choked her to death had not my friends intervened.

How like that lizard is the alcoholic cup! One begins to toy with cocktails, or other spiritous liquors, only to find that at the last the drink habit becomes so strong it masters the one who thought he could drink or let it alone as he pleased. Can any folly be greater than that of deliberately starting something which one knows he may have no power to stop, and yet he is fully aware that the matter in question may mean his moral, physical, and spiritual ruin?

Yet how many there are who think it an evidence of weakness to refuse to touch alcoholic beverages, and consider it a mark of good fellowship and even manliness to drink with the crowd and so win the approval of careless worldlings, who have no fear of God or of consequences in their hearts. These glory in leading others to follow their evil example and are never better pleased than when they can point to some poor, foolish youth who has begun to tread the downward path at their behest. Recognizing the fact that nothing that is physically harmful can ever be morally right, consecrated, Christian young manhood and young womanhood must stand firmly against all such wickedness.

"Lippen To" Jesus

"He that believeth on me hath everlasting life" (John 6:47).

Being of Scotch extraction, I always greatly enjoy the broad Scotch translation of the New Testament. In that you will never find our English word, "believe," but you will find the word "lippen." For instance, John 3:16 reads, "For God sae loved the warld as to gie His Son, the only begotten Ane, that ilka ane wha lippens till Him sudna dee, but hae life for aye." What does that word mean, the word "lippen"? It just means to trust your whole weight on a thing, trust it implicitly.

A Scotch minister was visiting a poor woman who was in great distress about her soul. She just could not seem to understand. By and by he left her, and on his way back to the manse he was troubled to think he had not been able to help her. He came to a bridge over a burn in front of the house, which he started to cross, going step by step very carefully with his buckthorn cane.

An old Scotch woman called out, "Why, Doctor Man, can ye no lippen the brig?" He laughed and waved his hand, and said to himself, "I have the word for my auld lady." So he went back to the cottage. She opened the door and said, "O Doctor, you've come back again?"

He said, "I have the word for you now."

"What is it, Doctor?"

"Can you no lippen to Jesus?"

"Oh, is it just to lippen to Him? Why, surely I can lippen to Him. He will never let me doon, will He?"

They bowed together, and she settled it. That is all God asks you to do. Believe the record He has given concerning Jesus; put your heart's trust in Him. You may be assured that you have life eternal for "He that hath the Son hath life; and he that hath not the Son of God hath not life. These things have I written unto you that believe on the name of the Son of God; that ye may *know*"—not merely hope, not just have a reasonable assurance, but full assurance—"that ye *have* eternal life."

Open The Door To Jesus

"Behold, I stand at the door and knock: if any man hear my voice, and open the door, I will come in to him, and will sup with him, and he with me" (Rev. 3:20).

An old woman was in great distress because of deep poverty. She was living in a little garret in London, England, and was dreadfully afraid the landlord and the bailiff would come to dispossess her, and perhaps, sell her bed from under her because of her debt. It happened that a certain Christian minister heard of her need and by interesting some friends raised sufficient money to go to her creditor and pay everything. Then, with the receipt in his hand, he went to see her. Her neighbors knew her only by the name, "Old Betty." When the clergyman arrived at the house, he said, "Can you tell me where Old Betty lives?"

They told him to go up the stairs to a certain room; he went up, knocked at the door and waited but there was no answer. He knocked again and still there was no answer. He called, "Old Betty, are you there?" but no answer.

He started down the stairs and was going away when the neighbors said, "Did you find her?"

"No, she is evidently not in."

"Oh, she's in all right, she just wasn't going to let you in," they said. "She's afraid to open the door."

And so he went up again and knocked and then one of the neighbors called, "Old Betty, let him in; it's the clergyman come to see you."

"Oh," the voice came from within, "I thought it was the bailiff and I wasn't going to open," and she opened the door and received the minister.

He said, "I have come to tell you that some friends have heard of your need and have paid all your debt. They have asked me to bring you the receipt, and here is a little gift to help for the future."

"Just to think," she said, "and I locked and bolted the door against you. I was afraid to let you in."

Is that not the way people are treating the Lord Jesus Christ? I am wondering whether you, unsaved one, have been treating Him like that. For years He has been knocking at your heart's door, He wants to come in to bring you peace and joy with the knowledge of sins atoned for and guilt put away, but you have bolted and barred your heart's door against Him, you have kept your best Friend out. But He is waiting still and continues to knock. Why not open your heart's door at once and receive the salvation so freely proffered?

Who Can Pay?

"When they had nothing to pay, he frankly forgave them both" (Luke 7:42).

Years ago, Nicholas, the First, Czar of Russia, was occasionally in the habit of throwing aside the garb of royalty, attiring himself in the uniform of a lower officer, and going about to find out how things were going with his soldiers. On one occasion he had a favorite, a young man, the son of an intimate friend of his, to whom he had given a position in a border fortress in charge of the money used for paying off the soldiers. This young man fell into bad habits; he took to gambling, and by and by, led on and on by the will-o'-the-wisp that lures the gambler to his doom, had gambled away all his own wealth and then had taken from the government funds entrusted to him. He had taken just a few rubles at a time and had no idea of the amount abstracted. He received notice that on the following day, an official was coming from the court to examine the records and to count the money he had on hand. He felt he never could face the exposure of that day and so the night before, closed his door and sat there with his books before him. He opened the safe, took out the pitifully small amount of money, counted it carefully, jotted down the amount on a sheet of paper, made note of the various peculations that he had abstracted, and when he had added it, he sat looking at it, and finally wrote under the figures, "A great debt; who can pay?"

He knew it was impossible for him ever to settle; looking at the small amount of money, he thought, "What a failure I have been!" He made up his mind that he would not live to face the disgrace of the morrow; he would blow his brains out as the clock struck twelve that night and leave all the papers so that the agent would understand all that had happened. As he sat there reflecting upon the way he had thrown away his opportunity, suddenly he felt him' self overpowered with drowsiness and in spite of the horror of his situation, went off to sleep.

It so happened that night, the Czar Nicholas, attired as a lower officer of the guard, entered the gate of that fortress, by giving the proper password, and moved down through the halls. Every light should have been out according to regulations but as he came down the main hall, he saw the light shining under a door. He went up to the door and listened but there was not a sound. He tried the knob, the door opened; he looked inside and saw the sleeping officer and then the money and the open safe, the papers, the books, and he wondered what it meant. He tiptoed in and stood behind the man, and looking over his shoulder, read the paper before him. The whole thing became clear in a moment. The young man had been stealing systematically for months.

The Czar's first thought was to put his hand on his shoulder and tell him that he was under arrest. The next moment his heart went out to him in compassion; he remembered his boyhood; he remembered the father; how broken hearted he would be if the son should be arrested! Then he happened to see that pitiful question, "A great debt; who can pay?" Moved by generous impulse, he reached over, picked up the pen that had fallen from the hand of the sleeping man, wrote just one word under that line, tiptoed out, and closed the door.

For an hour or so the man slept, then, wakened suddenly, he saw it was long past midnight. He sprang to his feet and picked up his revolver, put it to his forehead, and was just about to pull the trigger when his eye caught sight of that one word on the sheet of paper which he knew was not there when he went to sleep. It was the name, "Nicholas." Dropping his gun, he said, "Can it be?" He went to one of his files and got hold of some documents that had the genuine signature of the Czar and compared them with the one word written under the line, "A great debt; who can pay?" It was the real signature of the Czar and he said, "The Czar has been here tonight, he knows all my guilt and yet he has undertaken to pay my debt, I need not die." And so instead of taking his life, he rested upon the word of the

Czar as indicated by that name written upon the paper, and he was not surprised when, early the next morning, a messenger came from the royal palace bringing a sack of gold which he counted and found to be exactly the amount of the missing money. He placed it in the safe and when the inspector came and went over the books, everything was found to be all right. Nicholas had paid in full.

It is only a human illustration but it pictures what the Lord Jesus Christ has done.

"Jesus paid all my debt

Oh, wondrous love;

Widest extreme He met,

Oh, wondrous love.

Justice is satisfied,

God now is glorified,

Heaven's gate thrown open wide,

Oh, wondrous love."

One word spoke peace to that man's heart, "Nicholas." One word has spoken peace to my heart, the name, "Jesus." For through Him and His work upon the cross satisfaction has been made for all my sins. And for you, there is the same salvation, the same absolution, the same pardon, the same forgiveness, for God "hath made him to be sin for us, who knew no sin; that we might be made the righteousness of God in him" (II Cor. 5:21).

A Good Sinner

"There is no difference: For all have sinned, and come short of the glory of God" (Rom. 3:22, 23).

"Are you saved, sir?" we asked a gentleman at the close of a gospel-meeting.

"No, I really can't say I am, but I would like to be."

"Why would you? Do you realize you are a lost sinner?"

"Oh, of course, we are all sinners."

"Ah! but that often means little or nothing. Are you a sinner yourself?"

"Well, I suppose I am, but I'm not what you could call a bad sinner. I am, I think, rather a good one. I always try to do the best I know."

"Then, my friend, I fear there is little use seeking to show you the way of salvation. Good sinners, together with honest liars, upright thieves, and virtuous scoundrels are far from being ready to submit to the *grace* of God, which is only for poor, vile, hell-deserving sinners, who have no merits to build on, no goodness to plead, but who are ready to be saved alone by the work of Another, and that One the Lord Jesus Christ."

Further conversation but elicited the fact that the gentleman was far from being ready to be saved and would, according to his own declaration, rather take "his chances" as he was.

The Human Fly

"They ... weave the spider's web: ... neither shall they cover themselves with their works" (Isa. 59:5, 6).

Some years ago there came to Los Angeles, the great metropolis of Southern California, a so-called "human fly." It was announced that on a given day he would climb up the face of one of the large department store buildings, and long before the appointed time, thousands of eager spectators were gathered to see him perform the seemingly impossible feat.

But slowly and carefully he mounted aloft, now clinging to a window ledge, anon to a jutting brick, again to a cornice. Up and up he went, against apparently insurmountable difficulties. At last he was nearing the top. He was seen to feel to right and left and above his head for something firm enough to support his weight, to carry him further. And soon he seemed to spy what looked like a grey bit of stone or discolored brick protruding from the smooth wall. He reached for it, but it was just beyond him. He ventured all on a spring-like movement, grasped the protuberance and, before the horrified eyes of the spectators, fell to the ground and was broken to pieces. In his dead hand was found a spider's web! What he evidently mistook for solid stone or brick turned out to be nothing but dried froth!

Alas, how many are thinking to climb to heaven by effort of their own, only to find at last that they have ventured all on a spider's web, and so are lost forever.

"I'm In For A Good Time"

"She that liveth in pleasure is dead while she liveth" (I Tim. 5:6).

Some years ago, I had been preaching Christ as God's remedy for man's ruined condition, to the hardy population of a beautiful mining town in the mountain regions of Northern California. One afternoon I noticed in the meeting-hall a young woman whose sin-marked face, weary look and careless demeanor could not fail to attract attention.

Stepping over to her at the close, I asked, "What about your soul? Have you ever thought of preparing for eternity?"

"My soul?—I ain't got none," was the flippant reply, accompanied by a foolish laugh. Further conversation seemed to make no impression, for, after solemnly warning her of coming judgment, she exclaimed, "You ain't going to scare me into religion. Wouldn't I look nice joining you folks? I'm in for a good time——."

"But when you've had your day, when your so-called good time is over forever, when death, judgment, and eternity have to be faced, when God has to be met, *what then?*"

"Oh, well, of course, I don't intend to live like this right along. I'll get religion when I grow old. I ain't got time for it now."

"Yes; so the devil has deceived thousands, but you may never live to grow old. You may not have time to prepare for eternity, though you must find time to die."

Another laugh greeted this warning, and she was gone. It seemed almost impossible that so young a person could be so hardened. I was told she had abandoned herself to a grossly wicked life, though little more than a child, and was an outcast from respectable society. Alas, how sin degrades, hardens, and blinds its poor victims!

Some weeks after the above conversation, an undertaker came to the house where I was staying; he said that he had a funeral to conduct that was a source of much embarrassment to him. The person to be buried was a young woman of so notorious a character that he could scarcely persuade anyone to act as pall-bearers. Mentioning her name, he asked if we knew any who might do her this last service. We promptly offered ourselves. That would do. Some former companions of her folly had already promised to be the others.

It was the girl I had so recently spoken to, cut down in a moment—"suddenly destroyed, and that without remedy." Two days earlier, after a public holiday spent in a revolting manner, she was borne home drunk and put into a bed, from which she never arose. In a few hours she had passed into eternity, having died in great agony from the baneful effects of her long debauch. The wine-cup and its accompaniments had claimed another victim.

Awful was the sight of her pale, swollen face. A minister had been called in, but what could he say? What comfort could he give? Of death-bed repentance even he could not speak. No hope could he hold out that she might after all be saved. She had been asked by her mother if she wanted some one to come in to pray with her. "No," she said, "no one." "Couldn't she remember a prayer, then, to say herself—the Lord's prayer, or any other?" "No, I can't"; and instead of prayer there were oaths and groans of anguish. "She had lived her life," the minister said, "I shall not speak of it, for it cannot be altered now. You have *yours* to live yet. I speak then to *you*," and he faithfully urged them to flee to Christ alone for refuge.

As I helped to lower the coffin into the grave, my heart was sad indeed. As I turned away, I heard some one exclaim, under his breath, "Just think of it, only seventeen years old, and gone to—— !" The last word was lost in the noise about me, or perhaps never uttered.

Not Only Necessary—But Enough

"There is one God and one mediator between God and men, the man Christ Jesus; who gave himself a ransom for all to be testified in due time" (I Tim. 2:5, 6).

In a hospital ward a lady missionary found an undersized and undeveloped little Irish boy, whose white, wizened face and emaciated form excited her deepest sympathy. Perhaps he was of about fifteen years of age; he scarcely looked to be twelve. Winning the lad's confidence by gifts and flowers and fruit, she soon found him very willing, and even eager, to listen to the story of the sinner's Saviour. At first his interest seemed of an impersonal character, but gradually he began to be immediately concerned. His own soul's need was put before him, and he was awakened to some sense of his lost condition, insomuch that he commenced seriously to consider how he might be saved. Brought up a Romanist, he thought and spoke of penance and confessional, of sacraments and church, yet never wholly leaving out Christ Jesus and His atoning work.

One morning the lady called again upon him, and found his face aglow with a new-found joy. Inquiring the reason, he replied with assurance born of faith in the revealed Word of God, "O missis, I always knew that Jesus was necessary; but I never knew till yesterday that He was enough!"

It was a blessed discovery, and I would that every reader of these pages had made it. Mark it well: Jesus is enough! "Who of God is made unto us wisdom, and righteousness, and sanctification, and redemption." "Ye are complete in him." "God hath made us accepted in the beloved." These are only a few of the precious declarations of Scripture which show clearly that Jesus is indeed not only necessary, but enough.

It is believed by most people that Jesus is necessary. The whole fabric of Christendom is built upon that. But, alas, how few realize that He is enough!

You see, it is not Christ and good works, nor Christ and the Church, that save. It is not through Christ and baptism, or Christ and the confessional, that we may obtain the forgiveness of our sins. It is not Christ and doing our best, or Christ and the Lord's Supper, that will give us new life. It is Christ alone.

Christ *and*—— is a perverted gospel which is not the gospel. Christ without the *and* is the sinner's hope and the saint's confidence. Trusting Him, eternal life and forgiveness are yours. Then, and not till then, good works and obedience to all that is written in the Word for the guidance of Christians, falls into place. The saved soul is exhorted to maintain good works, and thus to manifest his love for Christ. But for salvation itself, *Jesus is not only necessary, but He is enough.*

The One Mediator

"To which of the saints wilt thou turn?" (Job 5:1).

My mother spent her last months on earth at Long Beach, California. My wife and I arranged to be with her so as to help in any way we could. Each afternoon I was in the habit of going down to the sands for a little rest and relaxation, and I always took my Bible with me.

While reading it one day, a young couple approached and, after introducing themselves, began to ask some questions about certain Scriptures. This led to a daily Bible study right on the beach. Eventually scores of people would gather with their Bibles and it was a joy to seek to open up the Word to them. For some weeks we studied the epistle to the Hebrews.

One day, as the meeting was closing, a warmhearted Irish woman, who had been sitting on the outskirts of the crowd, came over to me and expressed her appreciation of the message. She exclaimed, "I am a Roman Catholic and this is the first Protestant conventicle I have ever attended. I've seen ye each day as I went by, but I did not think I ought to listen, but as I was passing this afternoon I heard you say something so good about my dear Lord Jesus that I felt it would not be wrong to hear more—so I came close and I have enjoyed it all. You've told me things about my dear Saviour today I never heard in all my life before, and I am so glad I came."

I inquired, "You know Jesus as your own Saviour and Lord?" "Indeed I do," was the reply. "He's been my Friend for years, and since my husband died He's been like a husband to me, and a Father to my children. I go to Him about everything and He always answers my prayers and takes care of me. He died for me and I trust Him to keep my soul."

Perhaps a bit mischievously, I asked, "But do you only pray to Him? Don't you pray also to the blessed virgin and to the saints when you are in trouble?" I shall never forget her answer. "Oh, bedad!" she exclaimed, "What would I be after bothering with the virgin and the saints for, when I can *go* direct to my blessed Lord Himself!"

Would that all might realize the blessedness of this. Because He ever liveth, we are invited to "come boldly unto the throne of grace, that we may obtain mercy, and find grace in every time of need." The Lord Jesus is interested in all that concerns us. Why then turn aside to any other?

The Unsettled Past

"God requireth that which *is* past" (Eccles. 3:15).

A solemn instance of the danger of neglecting salvation came to my notice sometime ago. It is absolutely authentic.

An earnest evangelist, a personal friend of mine, was holding a series of meetings in a city in western Michigan. One night his text was Ecclesiastes 3:15. Faithfully he sought to show his hearers the impossibility of putting themselves right with God by reformation or human merit. Let the future be as it might, the past would have to be faced at the Great White Throne. Sin must be atoned for, and the guilty one could never atone for his own iniquity. He went on to show that God, in grace, had given Jesus to die, that His precious Blood was shed to put away sins, that all who trusted Him could say, "I have settled with God about my past now, for Jesus died for me. My sins are gone. He paid my debt. God requireth that which is past; but He has required it of Jesus, and my soul is set free."

In the audience sat a lady who listened with deepest interest. The day after the meeting she expressed herself as being concerned and anxious about her soul, but like many others, she procrastinated; and, instead of settling the matter at once, she chose to go on *unsaved.*

The next day she was drawing some gasoline for a customer in the little store where she worked. A lamp was near. Suddenly there was an explosion and then a mass of flame! She ran from the place, screaming for help. Neighbors came to her rescue, but it was too late to save her life. Conveyed to a hospital, she lingered some twenty-four hours and then passed into eternity.

As she lay in the ward, she was heard wailing hour after hour, "My sins! My sins! I haven't settled with God about my past!" Christian friends were there to point her to Jesus, who even now would save her if she accepted Him; but her agony was so great, none could tell whether she looked to Him or not. While *hoping* she had a saving glimpse of the One who died to redeem her, her loved ones could only leave her with God.

The incident illustrates the grave danger of refusing to close at once with Christ.

Have *you* settled with God about your past? Are yom sins washed away in His precious blood? If called as suddenly as she to face eternity, would your cry perhaps be as hopeless as hers? Oh, be persuaded, "God is not mocked: For whatsoever a man soweth, that shall he also reap." The loss of your soul is too terrible to be unconcerned.

"To lose your wealth is much;

To lose your health is more;

To lose your soul is such a loss

As no one can restore."

Come now to Jesus with all your sins; and owning your lost condition; trust in Him, while grace is free. "He, that being often reproved hardeneth his neck, shall suddenly be destroyed, and that without remedy" (Prov. 29:1).

The Conversion Of Thomas Scott, A Unitarian

"That all men should honour the Son, even as they honour the Father. He that honoureth not the Son honoureth not the Father which hath sent him" (John 5:23).

It is related of the eminent commentator of the eighteenth century, Thomas Scott, that he was for some years opposed to the precious and important truth of the deity of the Lord Jesus Christ. Like most Unitarians, the lower his thoughts were as to the Son of God, the higher they were as to himself and his own righteousness. A proud Pharisee, he fancied that he was quite able to save himself, if indeed he needed saving at all.

Through a careful, thoughtful study of the Scriptures (afterwards his food for forty years), he was awakened to see his lost condition and his deep need of a Saviour and Mediator. Relating his experience in *The Force of Truth,* he says: "I clearly perceived my very best duties, on which my main dependence had hitherto been placed, to be merely specious sins; and my whole life appeared to be one continued series of transgressions. I now understood the apostle's meaning when he affirms that 'by the works of the law shall no flesh be justified' before God" (Gal. 2:16).

Thus aroused, he saw that none but a divine Saviour could avail for so great a sinner as he now realized himself to be; and so, trusting in the Lord Jesus, he found peace and joy.

Unitarianism, like so-called Christian Science, Theosophy, and various other human religions, will do well enough for a man with a drugged or sleeping conscience; but the gospel of the grace of God alone can meet the need of an awakened sinner who has learned that God is holy and cannot look upon iniquity. To such there is a sweetness and healing balm in such words as John 3:16, of which the other knows nothing. "For God so loved the world, that he gave his only begotten Son, that whosoever believeth in him should not perish, but have everlasting life."

No Oil In The Lamp

"They that were foolish took their lamps, and took no oil with them" (Matt. 25:3).

Nothing is sadder than profession without possession; nothing more solemn than to have a name that one lives, while actually dead in trespasses and sins. Many are like this, they have no sense of their true condition.

The following case came to my notice while I was preaching in a middle western city, sometime ago. The lady related it to me herself. She had been for years a professor of religion, attending services frequently, reading her Bible with some degree of regularity, saying her prayers and attending to what she thought were her duties as one who belonged to a respectable church. In short, she was doing all she knew how in order to prepare her soul for eternity. But, while she hoped she was all right, she was never very seriously concerned for her conscience had not yet been reached and so, as she put it afterwards, she was contentedly hastening on to judgment, relying upon her own fancied goodness and meritorious works for salvation.

She was alone in her room one night when suddenly the lamp which had lighted went out, leaving her in the darkness. Almost involuntarily she exclaimed, "There is no oil in the lamp!" The words were scarcely uttered till they seemed to come reverberating back into her ears, but with a new and solemn meaning. "No oil in the lamp! I've heard that before. Ah, yes, the parable of the virgins (Matt. 25:1-12). Five of them had no oil in their lamps when the bridegroom came, and they were shut out of the feast." Her mind became troubled. For several days, and even nights, the thought was ever with her. She would often cry out in anguish of soul, "No, I have no oil in my lamp. What will become of me? I have not the grace of God in my heart!"

A horror of great darkness came upon her. She longed to be saved, yet knew not how. In great distress she began to pray, and God opened her eyes to see her utterly lost, undone condition in His sight, and showed her that she could do nothing to save herself. She searched His Word for light as to how she might obtain the longed-for "oil," and at last was led to realize that the work that saves had all been finished long ago when the Lord Jesus bore her sins in His own body on the tree (I Pet. 2:24); that all she had to do to possess eternal life and to *know* that she had it, was to believe on Him (I John 5:13). Glad she was indeed to be saved so simply, and yet in a way that brought such satisfaction. Sin had been all judged on Another, and she was justified from all things (Acts 13:38, 39). In simple faith she rested in Christ, and can now rejoice that she is His for time and eternity. Before she had profession, now she had Christ; before she was dressed in the rags of self-righteousness, now she was clothed in the righteousness of God (I Cor. 1:30); before she had an empty lamp only, now she was the possessor of the oil of the Spirit, who has sealed her for heaven (Eph. 4:30).

Praying Or Trusting

"As though God did beseech you by us, we pray you in Christ's stead, be ye reconciled to God" (II Cor. 5:20).

Visiting in a hospital not long ago, I spoke to a poor man of emaciated aspect, whom his friends had been anxious that I should see. He was evidently in a very precarious condition, possibly soon to be summoned from time to eternity. I told him I was anxious to know how he stood as to the great matter of his soul's salvation, and asked if he enjoyed peace with God.

"Oh," was the reply, "I'm all right as to that. *I'm praying all the time.*" And a look of intense self-satisfaction settled on his face.

"Well, my dear fellow, I hope you know what Christ had to do to save such sinners as we are and that you know Him as your personal Saviour."

"Oh, that's all right. I've known about Jesus for a long time. I've belonged to a church since I was a boy. I haven't any fear for I'm always praying."

"Well, you see, it is not enough to know *about* these things, and people are not saved by praying. Do you trust in the precious blood of Christ?"

A violent attack of coughing interrupted the conversation. When he was easy again, he said, "I can't talk more to you, sir. It excites me too much. But you needn't fear for me, for I won't forget to pray." With this he turned from me, evidently signifying that the conversation was over, so

I could do nothing but retire, leaving on the table some simple gospel tracts in the hope that, as he could still read, they might be used of God for blessing to him.

His case is, I fear, like that of many who put prayer, or other Christian practices, in the place of Christ, whereas the truth is, Christ first, then all these other things; or, in other words, life first, then the needs of the new-born babe. Saved people are surely praying people, but there are thousands of persons who pray who are not saved. The Pharisees prayed even long prayers, yet they were not saved.

Nowhere in His Word, does God ask people to pray for salvation. Nowhere is eternal life promised in answer to prayer. People in recognized relationship with God are taught to pray, as children making known their wants to a loving Father. In the case of the one apparent exception, Simon the sorcerer of Acts 8, to whom Peter says, "Pray God, if perhaps the thought of thine heart may be forgiven thee" (v. 22) it is that of a man by profession already a Christian. His own answer to the apostle is the proof that the secrets of his heart had been made manifest, and thus of his unfitness to pray, for he exclaims, "Pray ye to the Lord for me" (v. 24).

Sinners desiring salvation are throughout Scripture urged to trust, to believe, to have faith in the Son of God.

Paul's answer to the jailer's anxious inquiry, "What must I do to be saved?" is not that he should pray, or beseech God to help him, but is clear and simple, "Believe on the Lord Jesus Christ and thou shalt be saved." God has not one plan for one class of sinners and a different one for another. All who ever were saved in any dispensation were saved by believing the testimony of God. His present testimony is that Christ died for our sins, that He was buried and rose again, and He says, "If thou shalt confess with thy mouth the Lord Jesus, and shalt believe in thine heart that God hath raised him from the dead, thou shalt be saved" (Rom. 10:9).

We are not saying these things to hinder any soul in distress from crying to God, as the publican who cried, "God be merciful to me a sinner." But we warn any soul from putting his confidence in anything which, in the end, would only fail him; and what an awful thing to fail in a matter whose issues are eternal. "God be merciful to me a sinner" is the acknowledgment of need and guilt, but cannot give peace. The publican might have cried that forever and still have not so much as dared lift up his eyes to heaven had he not believed God's Word. The moment the testimony of God is believed, that "Christ also hath once suffered for sins, the just for the unjust, that he might bring us to God" (I Pet. 3:18), the soul enters into peace with God.

Instead of calling upon us to pray for salvation, God Himself is beseeching men through His ambasadors to be reconciled to Him. Through them Christ is pleading with sinners to trust Him.

Precious then to be able to say, "I am *trusting* all the time" instead of what this poor man in the hospital was vainly repeating.

Living The Christ Life

"Yet not I, but Christ liveth in me" (Gal. 2:20).

I was holding a series of evangelistic meetings in a church in Virginia. One evening, a visiting minister was asked to open with prayer. He said, "Lord, grant Thy blessing as the Word is preached tonight. May it be the means of causing people to fall in love with the Christ life, that they may begin to live the Christ life." I felt like saying, "Brother, sit down; don't insult God like that." But I felt I had to be courteous and I knew that my turn would come when I could set forth the precious truth as to God's way of salvation.

The gospel is not asking men to try to live the Christ life. If our salvation depended upon our doing that, apart from a second birth, we would all be just as good as checked through to hell. It is impossible for an unregenerate man to live the Christ life, no matter how much he may admire it as seen in Jesus, as it would be for one who had no sense of tune or of rhythm to live the Paderewski life or the life of any other great musician. One may enjoy music and admire musical ability who could never play or sing himself. It takes the soul of a musician to enable one to live a musician's life, just as it takes the eye and hand of an artist to be a painter or a sculptor.

When born from above, Christ dwells in our hearts by faith and as He lives out His life in us we are enabled to walk as He walked. There is no other way whereby we may live the Christ life.

Honest Doubt

"If we receive the witness of men, the witness of God is greater" (I John 5:9).

Often when pressing the claims of Christ upon men and urging them to believe the gospel, I have had them seek to parry by declaring that they could not believe, as they were honest doubters. I suppose there is such a thing as an honest doubter, but I dislike the expression when that which men profess honestly to doubt is the infallible Word of the living God. Tennyson has written,

"There is more faith in honest doubt, Believe me, than in half your creeds." I am not so sure that Tennyson was correct; certainly not if it is a question of doubting the truth of the gospel. I would not like to go home and tell my wife something and have her say, "Well, my dear, I am trying to believe you, but, honestly, I doubt you. I believe there is more faith in honest doubt than in being too sure you are not trying to put one over on me."

A lady said when I had explained the way of life as clearly as I knew how and shown her some plain, definite passages from the Holy Scriptures, such as John 5:24 and Matthew 11:28, "Well, I am trying to believe."

"Trying to believe whom?" I inquired. "It is God who has spoken in His Word. What do you mean by saying you are trying to believe Him?"

She saw her sin and her mistake and exclaimed, "Oh, I did not realize what I was saying. Yes, I can and I do believe what God has declared." And her soul entered into peace.

The Blood Counts For Something

"The blood of Jesus Christ his Son cleanseth us from all sin" (I John 1:7).

A friend of mine, himself an evangelist, lay for many weary months in a Roman Catholic hospital in the city of Oakland, California, because of injuries received in an automobile accident. On a nearby bed lay a young priest, evidently a sincere and earnest man, but he was greatly troubled in *view* of possible death. An aged priest came from time to time to hear his confessions, and to grant him absolution. My friend longed to speak to him, but found him very difficult to approach.

One day, however, as the older priest was about to leave, he overheard the young one say to him, something like this, "Father, it is very strange: I have done everything I know to do. I have sought to carry out all that the church has asked, and yet I have no peace. How can I be sure that God has put away my sins?"

The other looked at him compassionately, and then exclaimed, "Surely the blood of Christ ought to count for something!"

As though a flash of divine light had entered his soul, the young priest's countenance changed. He looked up eagerly to exclaim, "Ah, yes, it counts for everything. I can trust that."

And it was evident afterwards that his soul had entered into peace. Can you trust the precious blood shed by that Holy Son, who drank the cup of judgment for your sins upon the cross? If so, God declares that your sins which are many are all forgiven.

Thus, redeemed to God and justified, you will enter, as never before, into the inner meaning of the garden and the Cross.

"Gethsemane, can I forget,

Or there Thy conflict see,

Thine agony and blood-like sweat,

And not remember Thee?

When to the Cross I turn mine eyes,

And rest on Calvary,

O Lamb of God, my sacrifice,

I must remember Thee."

The Wrong Door

"I am the door: by me if any man enter in, he shall be saved" (John 10:9).

A young man who often listened to a great Scotch preacher wanted to be saved. He had a longing in his heart to know Christ as his deliverer and to know the blessedness of God's salvation; although he wept and prayed and sought, he could get no sense of forgiveness, no assurance that he was received by God. One night the minister preached on those words, "I am the door: by me if any man enter in, he shall be saved" and he showed that "any man" took in poor sinners, no matter how vile, how wicked, how corrupt they were. As he preached, he could see the cloud lift from this young man's face; at the close of the meeting, he came to the front and said, "I got in tonight."

"What do you mean," asked the preacher.

"Why, I got in at the open door tonight while you were preaching."

"I am glad to hear it. But why did you not get in before? You have been troubled for a fortnight and I have been trying to help you, and others have been doing their best to help you. How was it that you did not get in until tonight?"

"Well," said the young man, "I have been at the wrong door all the time. I have been knocking at the saints' door and I found it locked against me. I thought I had to become good enough for God to save me, but I said tonight, I will try the sinner's door, and when I came to it, it was open and I got right inside."

Salvation Altogether Of God

"Giving thanks unto the Father, which hath made us meet to be partakers of the inheritance of the saints in light" (Col. 1:12).

There is a story told of an old man who owned a little narrow lot with a poor miserable cabin on it. Lots in his neighborhood had been selling for fabulous prices and he felt that some day his place would make his fortune. By and by a millionaire came along and seeing the possibilities of that block, said, "I want the whole thing."

He sent his agent to buy the whole block; when he came to the old man, he said, "What is the price of your place?" As the old man had waited long for this opportunity, he priced it at what he thought was a tremendously big figure. "Very well," said the agent, "I will take it."

"When do you want it?" the old man asked.

"In about two weeks I will be around with the deed and you can be ready to sign it. Here is a thousand dollars to bind the sale," replied the agent.

The old man was simply delighted and thought, "Well, if somebody has bought this place who is able to pay all that money, I ought to fix it up a bit." And so he bought some paint and went to work painting the old cabin. He bought some glass to replace the broken panes, and for two weeks he worked on the cabin. When this millionaire purchaser and his agent brought the papers for him to sign, he was so nervous about it he could hardly hold the pen. He was surprised that the purchaser did not say anything about the shack and so he said, "You see how beautifully I have painted it up and have put in some new windows. It is going to make a nice place. I hope you will be very comfortable in it."

"Oh," said the millionaire, "but I didn't buy this place for what is on it, but for what I am going to put on it."

That is how God justifies the ungodly. It is not because of what He finds in men, but He saves them for what He is going to put in them, for what He is going to do for them. When they put their trust in Him, they get everlasting life, they are justified, and all their sins are forgiven. Then God proceeds to make them fit for His own blessed presence, and when we get home to heaven, we will give Him all the glory.

The Bible A Mirror

"If any be a hearer of the word, and not a doer, he is like unto a man beholding his natural face in a glass: For he beholdeth himself, and goeth his way, and straightway forgetteth what manner of man he was" (Jas. 1:23, 24).

I ran across an illustration the other day that I think pictures this admirably. An elderly gentleman, who was very nearsighted, prided himself on his ability as an art critic. On one occasion he was accompanying some friends through a large gallery and was seeking to display his real or fancied knowledge of pictures to these friends. He had left his glasses at home and was not able to see things very clearly. Standing before a large frame, he began to point out the inartistic features of the picture there revealed. "The frame," he said, "is altogether out of keeping with the subject and as for the subject itself (it was that of a man) it is altogether too homely, in fact, too ugly, ever to make a good picture. It is a great mistake for any artist to choose so homely a subject for a picture if he expects it to be a masterpiece."

The old gentleman was going on like this when his wife managed to get near enough to interrupt. She exclaimed, "My dear, you are looking into a mirror." He was quite taken back to realize that he had been criticizing his own face.

Now the Word of God is such a mirror. It does not hide our deformities. It shows us up just as we are. But we are not to be occupied with our old selves. The Spirit of God would turn us away from self altogether to occupation with the risen Christ, and as we are taken up with Him, we are kept from sin. It is when we get our eyes off Christ and become self-occupied or taken up with the world around us that we fail. And who of us does not so fail? We all have to confess our failures from day to day, but our ever living Saviour is not only our High Priest to minister all needed grace and help, but even when we fail to avail ourselves of that as we should, He is our Advocate still and the moment we fail, He takes up our case with the Father. Mark, it does not say, "If any man confess his sin, we have an advocate," but rather, "If any man sin, we have an advocate." The moment we fail He is in the Father's presence about us, and as a result of His gracious advocacy, the Spirit continues His work in our hearts, bringing us to repentance and confession, and "If we confess our sins, he is faithful and just to forgive us our sins, and to cleanse us from all unrighteousness."

The Righteousness Of God

"And be found in him, not having mine own righteousness, which is of the law, but that which is through the faith of Christ, the righteousness which is of God by faith" (Phil. 3:9).

I was talking to a large group at a college one day and an illustration came to my mind which I think all the co-eds understood. I said, "Just imagine one of you girls working your way through college. You have very little with which to do; your parents are not able to provide for you; possibly you have no parents. There is going to be some great affair and all are supposed to be nicely dressed for this occasion; you do not like to be shabby, but you have so little to go on. Then you see that at the five and ten cent store there is a splendid sale on dress material for ten cents a yard. You have only a few dimes, but you go down and get a few yards and try to make a nice little gown so that you can go to that function. But you have never had much training as a seamstress and you have a lot of trouble. However, you work away on it, trying to make it look respectable. Then one day Lady Bountiful visits you; you have always dreamed about her, but never expected to see her. She takes a kindly interest in you and says, "Look, I want you to go down town with me." You go, wondering why she should be interested in you, and then she takes you into one of the most beautiful outfitting establishments of the city. You are stirred as you walk up and down those aisles; as she stops at the dress section, she says, "Now, my dear, pick out any dress you please—a gown for yourself, any one that you like."

"Well, really," you say, "that seems too good to be true. I am afraid my taste would lead me to pick out something too expensive."

But she says, "Go right on—anything you want."

And so your fancy for color leads you to select a certain one and you say, "Well, I think that would be very becoming."

"All right," she says, and to the saleslady, "How much is it?" The answer is, "Seventy-five dollars."

"Oh," you say, "that price is altogether beyond a poor girl like me."

"But that is all right," she says, "you like it and you are going to have it."

Imagine the girl coming back to her little room, seeing the poor old figured goods at which she had been working so long. She gets the new one out and tries it on and parades up and down before the glass. Finally, she calls in the other girls and says, "Oh, now I shall be found not having my own dress, this poor inexpensive thing, but this beautiful gown that has been given to me so freely!"

Paul looked at it that way. He had been trying to work out his righteousness himself, trying to make a beautiful garment in which to stand before God; but when he got sight of the risen Christ, and learned that every believer is made the righteousness of God in Christ, he said, "Away with that thing of my own providing, now that I can be dressed up in the righteousness which is of God in Christ,"

Total Depravity

"The heart is deceitful above all things, and desperately (incurably) wicked" (Jer. 17:9).

Many object to the doctrine of total depravity on the ground that all men are capable of some good even if unsaved. All of us recognize the value of decency in behavior, of a kindly spirit, of generosity in caring for the needy, and similar virtues, which are frequently seen in unconverted and even positively godless men and women. How, then, it is asked, can they be said to be totally depraved? Dr. Joseph Cook, the great Boston lecturer of the latter half of the nineteenth century, answers this question with the following illustration:

He said he had in his home a very beautiful and valuable clock. It had an exceedingly handsome case, a very fine set of works, a nice appearing dial and elegantly finished hands. It was altogether a good clock to look upon but it had one fault. It simply would not, or could not, keep time. It had been gone over by many different clockmakers, but no one had been able to correct this fault. As a timepiece it was totally depraved!

Is not this like man, even at his best, if he has not been born again? There may be much about him that others can admire, but he is positively unable to do the will of the Lord, because his heart is utterly estranged from God, and therefore so far as holiness is concerned, he is totally depraved. Only the new birth—regeneration by the Word and Spirit of God—can enable him to keep in line with the divine will as laid down in the Holy Scriptures. However righteous he may appear in the eyes of his fellows, because of this fatal defect all his righteousness is as filthy rags in the sight of God.

The Fulness Of The Scriptures

"The barrel of meal wasted not, neither did the cruse of oil fail, according to the word of the Lord, which he spake by Elijah" (I Kings 17:16).

In this, the barrel and the cruse were like the Word of God itself, whether we think of the Scriptures as a whole, or any separate passage or text. No matter how often we may have read it, nor how many sermons we may have heard upon it, there is always more to be discovered, as we ponder it anew under the guidance of the Holy Spirit.

Evangelist Gibbud, the New York missioner of some fifty years ago, used to like to tell of the uncouth lad who attended a school in the lower east side district of that great metropolis. He was very fond of his teacher because of the kindly interest she had taken in him. One day he approached her desk, after school was in session, holding out a very dilapidated-looking orange in his dirty, grimy, little hand. "Here, teacher," he said, "is an orange I've brung yer. It's been squz some, but there's lots in it yet!"

So it is with every portion of the Bible. No one has been able to exhaust the priceless treasure it contains. There is always more to be obtained from it for the refreshment of the soul.

Simplicity In Prayer

"Be careful for nothing; but in everything by prayer and supplication with thanksgiving let your requests be made known unto God. And the peace of God, which passeth all understanding, shall keep your hearts and minds through Christ Jesus" (Phil. 4:6, 7).

We need to realize that our God takes a Fatherly interest in every detail of our lives and bids us bring everything to

Him in prayer. Nothing is too small for His concern and nothing is too great for His power.

Years ago, the Free Kirk of Scotland was holding a Synodical meeting in the granite city of Aberdeen and worshippers were flocking in from all nearby towns to participate in the services. An aged man was wending his way to the city on foot, when he was overtaken by a young theological student; the two walked on in company. Despite the difference in their ages, they had much in common, and so they enjoyed chatting together as they jogged on toward their intended goal.

At noontime they turned aside to a grassy copse and sat down to eat the lunch which each had brought with him, first giving God thanks for His gracious provision. Afterwards the aged pilgrim suggested that they pray together before continuing their journey. The young theologue was a bit embarrassed, but agreed, intimating that the elder man should pray first, which he did. Addressing God as His Father in all simplicity, he poured out his heart in thanksgiving, then uttered three specific requests: he reminded the Lord that he was very hard of hearing and if he did not get a seat well up to the front in the kirk he would get little out of the sermon that evening, so he asked that a seat be kept for him near enough to the pulpit so he could get the benefit of the message; secondly, he told the Lord that his shoes were badly worn and not fit for city streets; he pleaded for a new pair though he had not the "siller" to purchase them; last of all, he asked for a place to stay for the night, as he knew no one in Aberdeen and did not know where to look for accommodations.

By this time the student's eyes were wide open as he looked upon the old man with mingled disgust and amazement, thinking it the height of impertinence to burden Deity with such trivialities. When his turn came to pray, he delivered himself of an eloquent, carefully composed discourse, which in turn amazed his older companion, who saw in it nothing that indicated a making known of his needs to God the Father.

Proceeding on their way, they reached the kirk just as the people were crowding in; it was soon evident that there was no longer even standing room left. The student thought, "Now we shall see what becomes of his presumptuous prayers. He'll see that God has more to do than to use His time saving a seat for a poor, old, country man." However, someone came out and the old man was just able to squeeze inside the door, where he stood with his hand up to his ear trying to hear what was going on.

Just then, it happened that a young lady in a front pew turned and saw him. She called a sexton and said, "My father told me to hold our pew for him until time for the sermon; then, if he did not get here, to give it to someone else. Evidently, he has been detained. Will you please go back and bring up that old man who has his hand to his ear and is standing just inside the door." In a few moments, petition number one was fully answered.

Now, in Scotland, some folks always kneel for prayer, as the minister leads; others reverently rise to their feet. The old man was the kneeling kind and the young woman always stood. As she looked down, she could not help observing the worn soles on the feet of the kneeling worshipper. Her father was a shoe-dealer! At the close of the service, she delicately approached the subject of the need of a better pair of shoes, and asked if she might take him to her father's store, though closed for the night, and present him with a pair. Needless to say, her offer was accepted as graciously as it was made. So petition number two was answered.

At the store the lady inquired where he was to stay for the night. In all simplicity he answered, "I dinna ken yet. My Father has a room for me, but He has no' told me whar it is." Puzzled for a moment, she exclaimed, "O, you mean your Father—God! Well, I believe we have that room for you. We were saving our guestroom for the Rev. Dr. Blank, but a telegram came this morning saying he could not come, so now you must just come home with me and be our guest." And so the third petition was granted.

The next day the student inquired as to the outcome of the prayer and was astonished to find that God had heard and answered each particular plea. He is never too busy to heed the cries of His needy people. What we all require is more confidence in His love and more earnestness and directness in prayer.

Verbal Inspiration

"Now we have received, not the spirit of the world, but the spirit which is of God; that we might know the things that are freely given to us of God. Which things also we speak, not in the words which man's wisdom teacheth, but which the Holy Ghost teacheth; comparing spiritual things with spiritual" (I Cor. 2:12, 13).

Those who object to the use of the term "verbal inspiration" as applied to the Holy Scriptures, often speak of it contemptuously as the stenographic theory of inspiration, implying thereby that it puts God in the position of a business or literary man dictating to a secretary, who in turn transcribes the exact words the employer has uttered. In opposition to this, they point to the diversities of style among Old and New Testament writers and gather from this that such a theory as verbal inspiration is utterly absurd. They rather believe, if they accept inspiration at all, that God revealed the truth to different individuals and they set it forth in their own language according to the measure of understanding which they had.

Needless to say, this latter view would do away altogether with exactness in divine revelation, and any thinking person who has had experience in dictating to stenographers will realize how readily individual attainments of culture and understanding may be taken into account when using secretarial help.

It has been part of my responsibility for a great many years to dictate literally hundreds and thousands of letters, and also manuscript for many books, pamphlets and periodicals, and I have invariably found that it was important to keep in mind the mentality and education of my secretaries.'

I recall how, a number of years ago, I was preparing a book on the epistle to the Philippians. It was coming out serially in a monthly magazine. My publishers wired me that they were out of material and would like more within a few days. I was holding special meetings in a western city at the time and staying in a hotel. Having no other stenographic help at hand, I sought out the public stenographer in the hotel and she agreed to take dictation on a chapter or two of my book. I gave it to her as I would have done to my own well-taught secretary had she been with me. It was the first time I had ever used one in this capacity who knew absolutely nothing of the Bible, and I did not realize how strange many biblical terms must have seemed to her.

When she brought the manuscript to me it was with difficulty that I could conceal either my mirth or indignation. I was paying her by the hour and the manuscript was almost worthless. I had to go over all of it, making scores of corrections on every page, and then she had to do it all over again and, of course, I paid double for it. In the very beginning I noticed she had entitled the manuscript "Paul's Epistle to the Philippine Islands." Every theological term was misconstrued. "Propitiation" had been changed into "prostration" and other terms were represented by words that could not by any possibility have any reference to the subject in question. This taught me a great lesson. From that time on, when giving dictation, I have always taken into account the capabilities and the knowledge of Scripture of my secretaries.

It is impossible to be too grateful for a secretary who knows the Word of God herself and readily appreciates religious terminology. On the other hand, it is often exasperating when circumstances are different; and yet I have found that by a little care I can generally adapt myself to the understanding of the amanuensis. For instance, it is not necessary to say "propitiation" if the word "atonement" will do instead. I do not have to speak of "sanctification" if I can express the same thought by the words "set apart." And so it would be actually possible for my various secretaries to exhibit a style of their own in the matter which they prepared at my dictation!

In a far higher sense than this, may we not think of God accommodating Himself to the intelligence and culture of the writers of sacred Scripture, so that He expresses Himself in one way through a poet like David or Isaiah, and in an altogether different manner through a farmer like Amos, or a fisherman like Simon Peter. Thus you have remarkable diversity in Scripture, coupled with marvelous unity of thought, because "holy men of God spake as they were moved by the Holy Ghost."

The Ribbon Of Blue

"Speak unto the children of Israel, and bid them that they make them fringes in the borders of their garments throughout their generations, and that they put upon the fringe of the borders a ribband (ribbon) of blue .... that ye may remember and do all my commandments, and be holy unto your God" (Num. 15:38-40).

Blue is the heavenly color. The ribbon of blue on the border of the Israelite's robe was to be a constant reminder that he belonged to the God of heaven, and was responsible to so behave himself as to glorify his heavenly Master.

The story is told of a young dauphin, or crown prince, of France, who was placed under the care of an English tutor that he might be educated for his high and lofty station. The tutor often found it very difficult to control the young prince, who was very high-spirited and independent. Not possessing the authority to administer punishment to one in such an exalted position, the tutor finally hit upon a plan whereby he hoped to insure better behavior.

One morning he produced a purple rosette, which he fastened upon the jacket of the prince, explaining that as it was the royal color, it was to be worn as an evidence of his regal station. "If," said the tutor, "I ever find you behaving in an unprincely manner, I shall simply point to the rosette, and you will understand."

It proved to be a most effective method of discipline. Occasionally, the prince would indulge in an outburst of unseemly language or act in an unworthy manner. The silent appeal to the purple was enough to bring him to his senses and to procure an apology and a promise of better self-control in the future.

So believers today are responsible to behave in accordance with their heavenly relationship—to "walk worthy of the vocation wherewith they are called." The ribbon of blue is to be seen upon all our garments as we walk through this world to the glory of God.

Copper Nails

"When I kept silence, my bones waxed old through *my* roaring all the day long" (Psa. 32:3).

There is nothing that so takes the joy out of life like unconfessed sin on the conscience.

I once heard the late Dr. F. E. Marsh tell that on one occasion he was preaching on this question and urging upon his hearers the importance of confession of sin and wherever possible, of restitution for wrong done to others.

At the close a young man, a member of the church, came up to him with a troubled countenance. "Pastor," he explained, "you have put me in a sad fix. I have wronged another and I am ashamed to confess it or to try to put it right. You see, I am a boatbuilder and the man I work for is an infidel. I have talked to him often about his need of Christ and have urged him to come and hear you preach, but he scoffs and ridicules it all. Now, I have been guilty of something that, if I should acknowledge it to him, will ruin my testimony forever."

He then went on to say that sometime ago he started to build a boat for himself in his own yard. In this work copper nails are used because they do not rust in the water. These nails are quite expensive and the young man had been carrying home quantities of them to use on the job. He knew it was stealing, but he tried to salve his conscience by telling himself that the master had so many he would never miss them and besides he was not being paid all that he thought he deserved. But this sermon had brought him to face the fact that he was just a common thief, for whose dishonest actions there was no excuse.

"But," said he, "I cannot go to my boss and tell him what I have done or offer to pay for those I have used and return the rest. If I do he will think I am just a hypocrite. And yet those copper nails are digging into my conscience and I know I shall never have peace until I put this matter right."

For weeks the struggle went on. Then one night he came to Dr. Marsh and exclaimed, "Pastor, I've settled for the copper nails and my conscience is relieved at last."

"What happened when you confessed to your employer what you had done?" asked the pastor.

"Oh," he answered, "he looked queerly at me, then exclaimed, 'George, I always did think you were just a hypocrite, but now I begin to feel there's something in this Christianity after all. Any religion that would make a dishonest workman come back and confess that he had been stealing copper nails and offer to settle for them, must be worth having.'"

Dr. Marsh asked if he might use the story, and was granted permission.

Sometime afterwards, he told it in another city. The next day a lady came up and said, "Doctor, I have had 'copper nails' on my conscience too." "Why, surely, you are not a boatbuilder!" "No, but I am a book-lover and I have stolen a number of books from a friend of mine who gets far more than I could ever afford. I decided last night I must get rid of the 'copper nails,' so I took them all back to her today and confessed my sin. I can't tell you how relieved I am. She forgave me, and God has forgiven me. I am so thankful the 'copper nails' are not digging into my conscience any more."

I have told this story many times and almost invariably people have come to me afterwards telling of "copper nails" in one form or another that they had to get rid of. On one occasion, I told it at a High School chapel service. The next day the principal saw me and said, "As a result of that 'copper nails' story, ever so many stolen fountain pens and other things have been returned to their rightful owners."

Reformation and restitution do not save. But where one is truly repentant and has come to God in sincere confession, he will want to the best of his ability to put things right with others.

Magnifying Christ

"Christ may be magnified in my body, whether by life or by death" (Phil. 1:20).

It is the business of a Christian to so manifest the spirit of Christ in his life that men and women will fall in love with our blessed Lord. People generally know little about Christ, but a devoted life magnifies and glorifies Him, thus leading them to trust Him for themselves. A striking instance of this come to my notice some years ago when I was engaged in a special evangelistic campaign among the mission stations of northern Arizona where devoted workers were seeking to present Christ to the Navajo and Hopi Indians.

In company with Rev. Fred G. Mitchell, veteran Missionary to these neglected people, I went one day to the mission hospital at Ganado. There my attention was drawn to a Navajo woman who occupied a bed in one of the small wards. She could not speak any English and my Navajo education was limited to about half a dozen words, so we could not carry on any animated conversation. Standing near her, Mt. Mitchell told me her story.

In the desert some ten weeks before, the missionary doctor had found her in a dying condition. The real circumstances were so horrible I shall not commit them to paper. Her cries of anguish had drawn the doctor to the place where she had lain helpless for four days and nights without food or drink. By that time, her case seemed absolutely hopeless. She was paralyzed from the waist down, could not move about; gangrene had set in and she was in a most pitiable state. A cursory examination led the doctor to feel that her case was hopeless. But he wrapped a clean blanket about her filthy body, put her in his car and hurried her to the mission station. He learned afterwards that the Indian medicine man had pow-wowed over her for some forty-eight hours and then announced that she was possessed of an evil spirit that could not be driven out. It was best to get her as far away from the hogan as possible, as otherwise the demons would haunt the place where she died, making it unsafe for others to dwell there.

In the hospital, further examination convinced the doctor that an operation might possibly save her life, but it would be a most dangerous and delicate one, and with perhaps one chance in a hundred that she might recover. The little group of missionaries were called in for prayer and the doctor undertook the operation. Mr. Mitchell told me that for nine days and nights afterwards he kept the patient under almost constant observation. Finally her fever disappeared and it was evident that she was on the road to recovery. As consciousness returned and she found herself in the comfortable hospital bed, waited on by a kind, little Navajo Christian nurse and assiduously looked after by the doctor, she was filled with wonder and amazement. When able to speak, she inquired of the nurse,

"Why did he do this for me? My own people threw me out to die; nobody wanted me; and he came and brought me here and has brought me back to life. Why did he do it? He is no relative of mine. I am a Navajo, and he is a white man. I cannot understand why he should do all this for me."

The nurse replied, "It is because of the love of Christ."

"Love of Christ," she exclaimed. "I never heard of 'love of Christ.' What is the 'love of Christ?' What do you mean?" The nurse tried to explain, but felt she was not making it clear; so she called for one of the missionaries.

For some fifteen days after that, one missionary or another talked to the patient for a few hours each morning. In order to make her understand, it was necessary to go clear back to the creation and make plain why Christ came into the world. The young woman listened with deep interest, her large gazelle-like eyes searching the missionary's face constantly as if for confirmation of so wonderful a story.

Finally, when she seemed to be well on the road to life again and her mind was clear and bright, the missionaries thought the time had come to urge her to definite decision. So they held another little prayer meeting together and then once more Mr. Mitchell told the story of redeeming love and tenderly inquired, 'My dear younger sister, (which is the characteristic way of addressing a Navajo Indian younger than oneself) do you not now understand about the love of Christ? Can you not take this blessed Saviour for yourself? Will you not put your trust in Him, turning away from the idols of your people, and worship the one true and living God? He has come to earth in the person of His Son and now He asks you to trust Him for yourself."

In simple words he presented the claims of Christ for sometime, but there was no answer. The woman lay there perfectly quiet, but it was evident she was thinking everything over. After some little time the door at the other end of the ward was opened and the doctor looked in just to make sure that everything was all right with his patient.

She looked up and her bright eyes expressed the gratitude she felt as she softly replied in the liquid tongue of the Navajos, "If Jesus is anything like the doctor, I can trust Him forever." She had seen Christ magnified in a man and her heart was won.

Holding On To Spikes

"And the Lord said unto Noah, Come thou and all thy house into the ark; for thee have I seen righteous in this generation" (Gen. 7:1).

Noah, like Abraham, is a very striking example of one who has been declared righteous because of his faith. It was faith that led him to prepare an ark for the saving of his house, when there seemed no evidence of a coming flood. It was faith that led him to obey God and enter that ark, with all his family, when commanded to do so by God. Inside the ark all were secure until the deluge was over. They were kept by omnipotent power, The ark bore all the brunt of the storm. Noah and his household were shut in by God, who had Himself closed the door. The same hand that shut them in shut all the unbelieving antediluvian world outside. The ark was a type of Christ. All who are in Christ are eternally secure.

Suppose when the ark was completed God had said, "Now, Noah, go and get eight large, strong spikes and drive them into the side of the ark." Imagine Noah procuring these spikes and doing as commanded. Then when each spike was securely fastened, let us presume that God said, "Come thou and all thy house and take hold of these spikes, and all who hang on to the end of the flood will be saved." How long do you think Noah and the rest would have been secure?

I can imagine each one taking hold of a spike—then the waters rising as the rain poured down. In a few minutes they would have been soaked to the skin. Then think of the terrific strain on joints and muscles as the ark was lifted from the earth and began its perilous voyage through the raging waters. I think I hear Noah calling to his wife, "Mother, how is it going; is all well?"

And she calls back, "I'm holding on. Do pray for me that I may be able to hold out to the end!"

Soon poor Mrs. Ham would cry out, "It's no use, can't hang on any longer. I am going to backslide." And she would let go and be swept away by the flood. How long do you suppose it would be before every one of them would be obliged to let go and so go down to death?

Thank God, that is *not* a true picture of His salvation. He is not calling men to hang on to Christ. But just as Noah entered into the ark and found there perfect security, so every believer is in Christ and saved for eternity. It is not a question of our ability to hang on, but of Christ's ability to carry us safely through to the glory. He who has begun the good work in us will perfect it until the day of manifestation.

Possessing Our Possessions

"But upon Mount Zion shall be deliverance, and there shall be holiness; and the house of Jacob shall possess their possessions" (Obad. 17).

While God has blessed us with all spiritual blessings in heavenly places in Christ Jesus, many Christians fail woefully when it comes to the enjoyment of those things which are ours by divine bequeathment. Many of us have never really explored the good land which the grace of God has opened up to us.

All of Canaan was given to Israel by God before they ever set foot upon it, but, as they were about to enter under Joshua, He told them that every place that the sole of their feet should tread on should be theirs. As they went through the length and breadth and found out for themselves what God had given them, they took possession of city after city and district after district, but never until the balmy days of King Solomon did they really possess it in all its fulness. They soon lost their hold on it, however, because of sin and unbelief, but Obadiah tells us that, in a future day, the House of Israel shall possess their possessions.

That will be when the Lord Jesus Christ reigns in glory on this earth and Israel will be restored to God. For us as Christians there is a great lesson in all this, a lesson which we have been slow to learn, and that to our own great loss.

The story is told of a man who obtained by inheritance a beautiful country estate. As he lived in the city he thought it best to dispose of this estate and use the money he would obtain from it in some other way. Getting in touch with a widely known real estate firm, he instructed them to go out and make a careful examination of the house, outbuildings, and the land belonging to the estate, and write it up in such a way as to make it seem attractive to anyone who was looking for a home in the country. When all his instruction had been carried out, a representative of the firm brought in the draft of the advertisement, which they intended to insert in various papers. In this ad, the old home was described in glowing terms: the beautiful porches, the large hallway, the circular staircase, the drawing rooms, living rooms and sleeping apartments, and all the different appointments which made for a perfect country home. The billowing lawns, trees, shrubbery, gardens and contiguous farming ground were also pictured in language calculated to arouse the interest of anyone who desired such a country estate.

As the agent read the description, the owner of the estate listened carefully, making no comment. At the close, the agent inquired, "What do you think of that? That ought to sell it, do you not think so?"

The owner replied, "Well to be frank, I have changed my mind; I have decided not to sell. I have wanted a place like that all my life and I had no idea that this estate was just exactly what I have been longing for. Your description has shown me what a fool I would be to part with it. So I will pay you for the work you have done, but you need not make any effort to sell it; I will live there myself."

Doubtless, the agent was disappointed as he saw a large fee disappearing, but the owner had learned the value of his possessions and soon moved in and enjoyed what he had been so ready before to pass on to someone else.

Are not many of us like this man? In God's Word we have unfolded for us the riches of our inheritance in Christ, and yet we fail to enter into and enjoy that which has been purchased for us at such a cost.

The Hands Of The Saviour

"They pierced my hands and my feet" (Psa. 22:16). "What are these wounds in thine hands?" (Zech. 13:6). "Reach hither thy finger, and behold my hands" (John 20:27).

The wounds in the hands of Jesus will remain, I take it, throughout eternity as the marks of His love for us. When He left this world He bore the nail-marks and when He returns to reign He will be recognized by them as the very same Jesus who died on the cross for sinners.

Some years ago, a poor woman—baptized a Roman Catholic, was lying very ill in a city hospital. Fearing she must die, she was in great distress of mind because of the "weight of her sins pressing down upon her guilty conscience."

A sweet-faced nun, passing through the ward, was called co the bedside of this dying woman, and to her she told the story of years of sin and shame. The nun promised to get in touch with the parish priest and to send him to see her, so he might hear her confession and administer the last rites of the church.

In the meantime, a Christian lady was visiting the patients and came to the woman's bed and found her very ready to hear the gospel story of free and full salvation through the crucified and risen Saviour. Eagerly the poor, distressed one drank in the living water, came to Christ confessing her sins, and was soon rejoicing in the knowledge of forgiveness and acceptance with God.

When the priest arrived he found her as happy now as she had been miserable. But he at once began to make preparations to hear her confession and then to administer the last sacraments of the church. He begged her to make a good confession, that he might absolve her from all her sins and so prepare her for death.

She looked up earnestly and said, "Let me see your hand first." Thinking her mind was wandering, he pleaded with her again, as the time was getting short, to confess all her sins and obtain forgiveness. Once more came the insistent demand,

"Let me see your hand first, father." In order to humor her, he held up his hand. She took it in one of hers and felt it carefully; then she exclaimed,

"It won't do, father. The hand of the One who forgives all my sins has a nail-print in it."

As she was deaf to all entreaties to confess to him, the priest left, feeling her case was hopeless. But instead of that, hers was a sure and certain hope, founded on the Word of God, "To him give all the prophets witness, that through his name, whosoever believeth in him shall receive remission of sins" (Acts 10:43). She bore a faithful testimony to saving grace and died triumphantly.

"The hands of Christ seem very frail,

For they were broken by a nail.

But only they reach heaven at last,

Whom those frail broken hands hold fast."

Hasty Conclusions

"Judge not, that ye be not judged" (Matt. 7:1).

The folly of snap judgments of others is well illustrated by a story the late Bishop Potter of New York used to tell on himself.

He was sailing for Europe in one of the great trans-Atlantic liners. When he went on board, he found another passenger was to share the cabin with him. After going to see his accommodations, he came up to the purser's desk and inquired if he could leave his gold watch and other valuables in the ship's safe. He explained that ordinarily he never availed himself of that privilege, but he had been to his cabin and had met the man who was to occupy the other berth and, judging from his appearance, he was afraid that he might not be a very trustworthy person.

The purser accepted the responsibility of caring for the valuables, and remarked, "It's all right, bishop, I'll be very glad to take care of them for you. The other man has been up here and left his for the same reason."

One is reminded of the lines of Robbie Burns, "Oh, wad some power the giftie gie us, To see oursel's as others see us." It is very easy to form snap judgments, only to find out afterwards that they are utterly unfounded. "Love believeth all things, hopeth all things."

Made in the USA
Middletown, DE
25 August 2025